FISH COOKERY

F I S H
COOKERY

Russ Lockwood

LYONS & BURFORD, PUBLISHERS

Design by Richard Oriolo
Printed in the United States of America

10 9 8 7 6 5 4 3 2 1

Library of Congress Cataloging-in-Publication Data

Lockwood, Russ.
    Fish cookery / Russ Lockwood.
       p.   cm.
    Includes indexes.
    ISBN 1-55821-246-9 :
    1. Cookery (Seafood)   I. Title.
TX747.L63   1993
641.6'92—dc20   93-28782
                                             CIP

CONTENTS

v

ACKNOWLEDGMENTS

Thanks are due most of all to Terre, my wife, without whose patience, understanding, and computer skills (not to mention the cast-iron stomach of a guinea pig) the whole project would have been the wrong kind of joke. We had a lot of fun collecting these recipes and hope others find as much enjoyment.

But thanks must also be extended to the many others who contributed recipe ideas and criticisms, as well as encouragement during the writing. In particular, I would like to express my deep gratitude to Dr. Walter Whitworth of the University of Connecticut—teacher, friend, and gourmand. The fishermen friends who gave freely of their time, knowledge, and sometimes fish, are too many to list, but are not forgotten. Thanks to you all.

Finally, special thanks must go to Coleen Webb, whose illustrations grace this book.

AUTHOR'S NOTE

Forty odd years ago I was awarded seven dollars—second prize in the National Forest Essay Contest—probably for the phrase, *"Remember, only YOU can prevent forest fires."* You may have heard it. (Last I knew, Bob, the first prizewinner, was a Senator.)

Since then there hasn't been much this native Vermonter found worth writing about. But over the last few years so many people have beat on me to collect my fish recipes into a book that I finally had to surrender and do it. The next time—if there is one—they can damn well copy my notes and do their own collecting and indexing! Good eating, good laughter, and . . . share water* (safely, of course).

---

* Robert A. Heinlein, the Mozart of science fiction, journeyed on his own "Glory Road" in 1988. The work of his fertile mind has amused, astonished, and sometimes challenged his readers since the 1930s. His revolutionary *Stranger in a Strange Land* expounds a philosophy of love and sharing that we should all Grok. I borrowed the phrase "share water" in tribute to this work of the master.

INTRODUCTION

C an I transmit the excitement of fishing to you? No! It's like riding a bicycle: you either do it or you don't. But eating—ah! . . . that's an almost universal sport. People who don't fish can still enjoy and benefit from eating fish. And the better the fish is prepared, the more enjoyable the sport is. That's where this collection of recipes comes in: trying to make both the preparation and the consumption more fun. For seasoning, some humorous (I hope) anecdotes and some serious general tips are included.

Reader convenience plays the major role in the organization of the chapters. Organization is not rigid in a technical sense (for example, some fish may be found in either fresh or salt water), so use the index to find a particular fish if it is not where you expect to find it. Chowders and soups are themselves such a large subject that they require a chapter of their own. Also, the cleaning and preservation of fish are subjects that deserve separate emphasis. Pastries and batters, required in many recipes, are easiest to find if grouped in one place—arbitrarily, the Fishellaneous chapter.

There are certain basic tips that you should be aware of before you go into the recipes.

1. Cholesterol exists. Try to avoid it as much as possible. Use low-fat milk, vegetable shortenings, margarine, and yogurt unless one of the old baddies is essential. For instance, lard is necessary for good pastry, salt pork is far better in most chowders, and a little butter mixed in with margarine often gives a better taste to herb butters.

2. Play with the recipes. The proportions of ingredients in most dishes are not rigid. Likewise, the particular ingredients usually can be varied to create different effects. I have had New England clam chowder made with anything from heavy cream (too thick) to skim milk (not bad at all). One mild-flavored white fish can usually be substituted for another.

3. What is an average serving? When I was fourteen years old I could eat five bowls of chowder and a couple dozen clam cakes. Now a bowl of chowder and two or three cakes is plenty. My father, in his seventies, still eats three times as much as I do. Look at serving sizes with a large grain of salt substitute. Any resemblance to appetites, living or dead, is pure serendipity.

4. Use clear glass baking dishes. They are valuable for cooking fish because you can lift a dish up to see from the color of the fish how done it is.

5. Use heavy cast-iron utensils. They heat uniformly and don't shed Teflon molecules into the food.

6. The shells of most bivalve shellfish should be tightly closed before cooking. If they are not, tap the animal lightly—if the shells pull tighter, the animal is healthy; no movement is one indication of a dead or moribund fish. If the shells do not open when cooked or if there is an odor, discard them.

7. Fresh fish of any kind has no offensive odor. If there is an objectionable odor, then the fish is suspect.

8. Color can also be an important indicator of freshness. If the flesh is dark or gray in color, it is probably not good. However, some fish, such as Bluefish or

Bluefin Tuna, are naturally dark, so best to ask someone knowledgable if in doubt.

9. If the fish is whole, look him in the eye. If the eyes are heavily filmed, the fish is not too fresh. Experts can judge a fish by its eye condition; cataracts never have been considered an indication of extreme youth.

10. Slimy fish are like slimy politicians—to be avoided.

11. Proper cleaning and storage is essential for high quality. Detailed discussion of the important steps follows in Chapter 1, but in brief: ice fish immediately and clean it as soon as practical. In some species of fish, such as the sharks, it is also necessary to *immediately* bleed and eviscerate the animals; uric acid in the blood will impart an ammonia taste and smell to the final dish if this is not done.

12. Fish spoils very quickly, especially at room temperature. Keep fish dishes hot or iced, depending on the type of dish.

ONE

· · · · · · · · · ·

CATCH CARE

N ot everyone is going to go out and capture his/her (Sorry, we seem to be short a unisex possessive pronoun) own seafood. But even if someone else catches it, it's a good idea to know how to save and clean the fresh seafood that comes your way—be it gifts from neighbors or something your child catches on your next vacation. So here are some pointers on how to keep those delectable critters as fresh as possible, and how to clean them in the neatest, easiest way I know.

SAVING THE CATCH

Keep your fish, shellfish, or crustaceans alive if you possibly can until time to clean or cook them. If removing the animal from the water will be fatal, then pack it loosely in cracked ice. Ice retards metabolism in crabs, lobsters, and clams, and keeps the animals alive longer. For cod, pollock, and shrimp, ice keeps spoilage bacteria from working as quickly as they would at ambient temperatures. Don't make the Sunday fisherman's mistake of leaving the catch lying in the sun in a burlap sack or a plastic can; I have watched too much excellent food turn to garbage that way. Another step toward better eating is to eviscerate—or at least bleed—finfish *at once*. Bluefish, for example, is almost totally inedible if not bled at once and iced. Even cod—one of the most forgiving of food fish—is far better when its organs are extracted *post haste*.

The best way to keep fish alive is to keep them in the water until you go home. On large party boats this is not practical because you can't reach the water to keep them there—besides which, blue sharks do enjoy market-size morsels. Holding baskets are a wise investment for the serious fisherman.

Fresh water kills salt-water animals, so don't pack those expensive crabs or lobsters where they will drown in melted ice (fresh water) before you reach your destination. Insulate them with seaweed and use ice in sealed containers to extend their life expectancies. (I learned this the hard way—twenty miles of backpacking a lobster into the deep woods, only to learn that a mountain spring is not a preferred lobster habitat.)

CLEANING THE CATCH

"You caught it, you clean it" is one of the first coherent thoughts I can remember from childhood, possibly because of endless repetition. Since a liberally applied two-by-four seems to be the only other way to get through to a mule or a young boy, and I can't find any scars, repetition seems at least a good suspect. The principle is a good one—even though few people have *really* experienced a hamburger (ground cow, big brown eyes and all).

The family of fish, like Julius Caesar's Gaul, can be divided practically into four parts: shellfish, crustaceans, cartilaginous fish, and teleosts (bony fish). The first two groups of animals wear their skeletons outside their bodies (squid and octopus are, of course, exceptions) while the latter two wear internal support. Shellfish have one or no joints in their shells (except certain slugs, which have overlapping armor plates) while crustaceans have articulated joints. Cartilage forms the support for shark and skate muscles while bone is the mainstay for the majority of finned fishes. But for cleaning, it is easiest to separate them simply into finned and finless fishes.

CLEANING FINLESS FISH

SQUID

What kind of tipsy topologist was responsible for calling the squid a member of the mollusks? Mollusks have external skeletons, while squid have only an internal "pen" (a tube of cartilage). But biology books insist that squid are mollusks. Oh well, I just eat here.

Clean a squid by popping its pen (the "external" skeleton, found internally) and exorcising its organs. The edible part of a squid is the saclike outer skin. The pen and organs are easily extracted and discarded.

BIVALVES

Two shells (or valves) held together by a hinge (umbo) with an animal inside defines a bivalve. But treatment of bivalves varies considerably according to the specific creature. For example, never cook an oyster to open it, but always steam mussels to open them. Bivalves are more tender if you can open them without cooking. My preferred trick for hardshell clams is to first freeze them and then let them partly thaw so the valves gape open slightly and I can insert a knife to cut the muscle. An old fashioned can/bottle opener is a choice tool for opening oysters (I have scars that contraindicate the use of a knife); lever the umbo apart with the rounded end of the opener.

Unless you are specifically fond of grit, scrub the shells of bivalves under running water before you open them. Similarly, pull the beards (byssal threads) off mussels before you cook them, or prepare for some serious chewing.

7

SNAILS

A single, unarticulated (jointed) shell generally defines a snail; but these vary from the tiny periwinkles of the New England coast (which make great spaghetti sauce) to the enormous Queen Conch of the Caribbean. Cleaning procedures are aimed at getting the animal from its shell so that you can cut away the dark stuff (intestinal tract) and enjoy its closer acquaintance. For the smaller and less decorative forms, cleaning is simple: break off the original part of the shell (they grow outward in spirals so it is easy to identify the original) to loosen the animal's grip on its shell and pull it out. Large, decorative conch shells are valuable, so this option is not so desirable. The easiest method I have found for the larger animals is to boil them in their shells and then extract them from their shells, even though this necessitates several passes through a meat grinder afterward. Freezing and partial thawing is another method of loosening the creature's grip on its shell, but whether or not that gives a more tender product is hard to judge.

CRUSTACEANS

Lobsters, crabs, shrimp, and prawns are probably the most widely consumed of fish life. Lobsters and crabs are usually marketed and cooked alive—notable exceptions being the Alaskan King Crab, which may easily reach the size of a room, and the single claw harvested from the Florida Stone Crab. Shrimp and prawns are usually marketed deheaded but unpeeled; they are cooked either peeled or unpeeled depending on the dish.

The best way to clean lobsters and crabs is, in a word, to pick. After the animal is boiled (the usual way for at least preliminary cooking), roll it over and open it from the stomach side. Split the lobster shell to get at its stomach parts; pull the pointed apron to separate the crab shell into parts. Discard the stomach contents unless you want to save the green stuff (tomalley) found in female lobsters for stuffing. (To sex a lobster when you buy it, look at the underside of the body where the jointed part of the shell joins the solid part of the shell. The little flippers on the first joint are soft in females and hard in males.) What remains after you empty the body cavity is meat, membrane, and gills. It's easy to tell which is the meat—it's the chewable part. With lobsters, picking out the meat and discarding the gills is relatively simple, but not with crabs. There are membranes separating the separate muscles in the main body. Pick each piece of meat out from the membranes as best you can—I suspect that is why the price of crabmeat is so high.

Shrimp and prawns can be cleaned either raw or cooked. Just peel off the outer shell and remove the vein running down the back. That is, of course, if you are buying the deheaded variety.

CLEANING FINFISH

The key to successfully cleaning finfish is understanding their anatomy. There are basically two body types: fusiform (torpedo-shaped) and flat. All finfish carry their viscera surrounded by bone (or bonelike) baskets—rib cages, so to speak. All possess backbones, although the "bones" of a shark or skate are actually cartilage. Fins can work only if bones support them from the backbone. Usually there is a visually prominent line (called the lateral line) running the length of the fish—a very sensitive sound sensing system which probably makes schooling behavior possible and which may also be linked to the backbone. These are the major bones, although salmon, trout, pickerel, and herring possess additional bones that make filleting impossible (at least for most of us). It is easiest to cook trout whole and lift the meat off the bones; to pickle pickerel or herring to dissolve the bones; and to buy filleted shad from one of the few ladies along the Connecticut River who know the secret boning procedure. Otherwise, almost any fish is best cleaned by filleting and subsequent skinning.

A typical fish

FIGURE 1

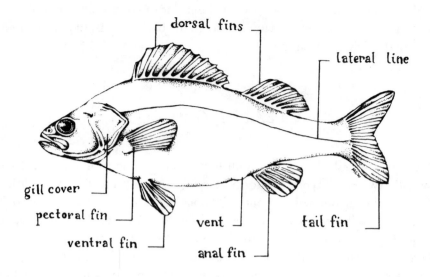

FIGURE 2

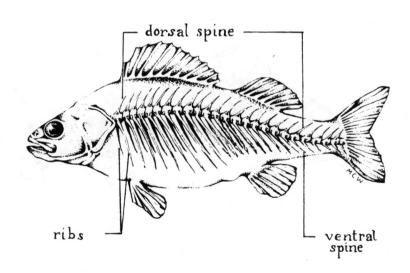

FIGURE 3

FILLETING FUSIFORMS

Figure l shows a typical fish. Figure 2 is a simplification of Figure 1, showing only features pertinent to cleaning. Vertebrae from the head of the fish to the anal fin (the fin that sticks out of the bottom of the belly) are shaped like an inverted Y, where the arms of the Y form the rib cage and the leg of the Y points straight up to support the dorsal (back) fin. From the anus to the tail there are no viscera, so the vertebrae become I shaped. Figure 3 illustrates this bone structure.

To clean this type of fish, lay it on a board and make a cut just behind the gills from the back to the lateral line (see Figure 4). Be careful to cut just to the bone, not through it.

Insert the tip of the fillet knife (edge out, parallel to the back fin) into the top of the cut. Work the knife tip slowly back toward the tail, keeping alongside the dorsal fin. When you reach the tail, go back to the head and insert the blade tip (edge in, parallel to the back fin). Keep the blade next to the bone and work it toward the tail. Bring it to the lateral line until you reach the anal fin, then slide the knife blade all the way through and sweep it back to the tail, freeing the fillet from the rib cage back (see Figure 5).

The meat on the rib cage is thin, so I usually grasp the fillet and pull it away

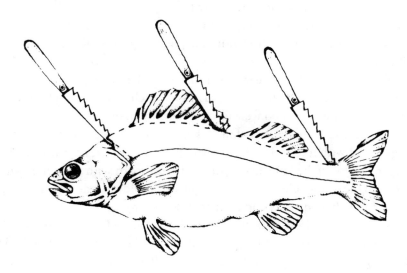

FIGURE 4

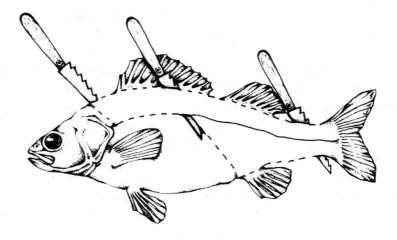

FIGURE 5

from the body of the fish to where I can cut it loose around the visceral cavity. With larger fish, such as cod, it is possible to actually pull the meat from the rib cage with the fingers, an art acquired only through practice.

Flip the fish over and remove the fillet from the other side in the same manner. Head, viscera, bones, and fins are left in one piece (at least in theory), permitting easy disposal.

Feel along the lateral line of each fillet for bones. Excise any residual bones by cutting through the meat down to the skin in a *V* to include the line of bones. When you skin the fillet, the line of bones will automatically be separated for easy discard.

Referring now to Figure 6, lay a fillet (skin side down) on a cutting board and, grasping the tail with the left hand, cut through the meat (but not the skin) beside your fingers. Holding the knife blade parallel to the board with a slight downward pressure, pull the skin while wiggling it slightly from side to side. This action peels the skin from the fillet quickly and accurately. Repeat for other fillets.

Always check the skinned fillets carefully for bones before setting them aside for cooking. It is easy to miss little pieces of fin, rib cage, or lateral line bones in the cutting. Running the tip of a finger over the likely places for a bone is quite effective in finding these residuals. Bones are much more likely to reside near the head end of the fillet, usually along the lateral line.

FIGURE 6

LATERALLY FLATTENED FISH

Laterally (side-to-side) flattened fish, such as members of the sunfish and porgy families, are handled in the same manner as fusiforms. For some unexplained reason, the scales of these flattened fish seem to run much larger than those of their streamlined cousins—important for the person sharpening the fillet knives and for kitchen cleanup (if the "gross" activity of cleaning fish is allowed in your domicile). Porgies have a full set of lateral line bones in the dark strip of meat that separates the lighter back and stomach portions of the fillet; be sure to cut these out.

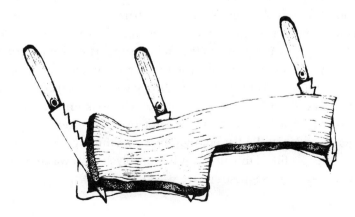

13

CATCH CARE

FIGURE 7

FLATFISH TRIBES

It would appear that sometime in the evolutionary past a genetic steamroller passed over part of the fish world, leaving one group so dorso-ventrally (back-to-front) flattened that both eyes are on the same side of the fish. This is not such a disadvantage to the fish as you might suspect, since these fish typically lie mostly buried on the bottom of the sea, blind (light) side down, and wait for dinner to deliver itself. The angler (monkfish, goosefish, etc.), while not a true flatfish, waits aggressively with a wormlike barbel dangling above its incredibly large and well-dentured mouth. Skates and rays—also not true flatfish—spend considerable time cruising about, looking for prey. Even members of the true flatfishes—such as halibut and fluke (summer flounder)—exhibit fiercely aggressive behavior at times; a halibut once followed my jig about forty feet off the bottom before attacking it; unfortunately, the fish probably weighed two or three hundred pounds while my line had only thirty-pound strength (such a short acquaintance, alas).

Cleaning the various uplookers can be divided into three categories: anglers; skates and rays; and flounders.

Anglers. Imagine a tub of gelatin with a mouthful of teeth running halfway around the tub, then add a barbel (a little dangler that looks much like a worm) and a disproportionately small tail—this is a monkfish. All the edible meat is in the basal part of the tail; it consists of two tubes of muscle (one on either side) of the backbone. Cut the tail off where it joins the large part of the body and skin it to reveal these fillets. Cut them from the backbone and remove the membrane covering the meat (the membrane is bitter and tough). I cut the fillets into half-inch-thick discs for poaching. Don't worry about the jiggly texture of the meat; cooking firms it.

Skates and rays. The edible portion of these animals is in the wings on either side of the thick central part of the body. Cut off the wings and give the central portion to your local friendly lobster fisherman for bait (the one who gives you the best deal on lobster). An irregular membrane runs through the middle of the wing parallel to the faces and provides the skeletal support so that the fish can flap its wings and "fly" through the water. The membrane divides the meat into two distinct sheets of muscle. To fillet the fish, simply cut the sheets of muscle loose from the membrane. But now comes the difficult part—skinning. Because sharks and skates have dendrites (little teethlike protrusions) instead of scales, it is difficult to get the fillets to lie flat enough for easy skinning. The dendrites give such a bumpy ride to a fillet knife that you'll probably end up wasting a good part of the meat—at least I do. Suggestions are welcome.

Flounders. From windowpanes (so thin you can almost see through them) to gigantic halibut (the largest on record is a 760 pounder brought into Boston in the 1800s) members of the flounder tribe are delicious. Their bone structure is also so simple that they are probably the easiest of all finfish to clean. Small flats are scaled and cooked whole (no meat wasted by filleting); giants are usually cut into steaks (I have filleted fish up to fifty pounds, and the pieces were incredible—a two-hundred-pounder would produce truly awesome fillets), but most flounders are filleted.

At first glance the flounders might appear much the same as sunfish, but this is only an illusion. The fins of flounders are actually pectorals (refer again to Figures 1 and 3, earlier). The dorsal spine has been truncated to a "process" (a biologist term for a bump) on the vertebrae and the lateral line bones have extended to become the main skeleton. So don't try to fillet the flounder in the same manner as a round fish; it won't work. The bump on the vertebrae will push the knife blade up and away from the bones, hence wasting meat. The trick is to cut down to the backbone along the lateral line, then slowly ease the cutting edge of the knife over to the horizontal, following the skeletal contour. It is then a simple matter to cut the two fillets from one side of the fish, flip it over, and repeat the operation on the other side. It is easiest to begin on the dark side (the "force" willing).

STORAGE OF FISH

Any time you have more than enough fish for the current meal, you face one of the oldest problems: how to store it in an edible condition for later. Probably the oldest technique is to lay the fish out in the sun and let it dry; this method is still used—in Nova Scotia you can see acres of racks with codfish fillets drying in the sun. The next attempt at preservation probably came about when some primitive man noticed that salt is great for retarding spoilage; those wooden boxes of salted codfish are still available at local grocers. (If you learned to loathe salt codfish in cream gravy over mashed potato as a child, don't feel all alone.) But then some enterprising genius discovered that smoking made an edible fish last quite a while (more on this later). Next came the Mason jar and the beginning of modern canning (unfortunately with some hazard, as pressure canning is necessary for

15

fish—a later discovered fact). Then came modern refrigeration (behold the frozen fillet, best known of all fish). Finally, desiccators modernized solar drying. Let's take a look at the advantages, disadvantages, and practical procedures for each of these storage techniques.

SOLAR DRYING

Properly dried fish will keep almost indefinitely, but it needs to be reconstituted with water or some other liquid to be used. The dried fish can be flaked into soups or soaked and then used in casseroles. The great disadvantage is that sun drying is a long and sensitive process. The fish is much more apt to rot than to be preserved unless you are an expert at this type of preservation. Briefly, the procedure is to spread the fillets (skin side down) on racks in the sun and to wait, hoping that there's no rain and that there is enough breeze blowing over the fish to let it dry. Good luck!

SALT PRESERVATION

Salt, by itself, can be used to preserve meat, as old time sailors were well aware. Other than the obvious contemporary implications of hypertension, the problem is that the product is not the most desirable—at least not to my taste. Even boiling the fish to remove most of the salt doesn't quite make it. I knew a hermit who packed his freshwater fish into a barrel with salt for later consumption; the last I heard he was still alive after many years of keeping his catch this way.

SMOKING

Historically, smoking may have been one of the earliest methods of preserving fish. The technology is somewhat improved today, but the process remains basically the same. The advantages of smoking are that it is simple and reliable, and requires a minimum of preparation or attention. The disadvantages are that the fish doesn't keep indefinitely, and that some people don't care for the taste, not to mention the fact that a lot of smoke is probably not going to be very good for you either.

Three things are of primary importance in making really good smoked fish: (1) the fish must be first quality; (2) the brining water must be pure (if it is chlorinated or otherwise treated, boil it first); and (3) the smoker must be able to maintain cool smoke temperatures over a long period. The first two factors are obvious with the additional note: *never use iodized salt to make the brine.* The third factor is easily achieved by building a smoker from an old refrigerator, a hot plate with a temperature sensor, an iron skillet, and some hickory chips. Build a closable vent into the refrigerator, set the hot plate in the bottom of it with the pan full of chips, adjust the thermostat on the hot plate, and plug the hot plate into an outlet. Put the brined fish on the racks and smoke to taste.

To make a good fish brine, dissolve noniodized salt in water in a glass or ceramic crock (1 cup salt to 1 gallon water makes a saturated solution). Soak the fish overnight, holding it under water with a weighted plate or equivalent. Less soaking time gives a less salty product, but this is mainly a matter of taste. Likewise, you may want to add seasonings to the brine or use something else to achieve a different effect—for example, I like to soak bluefish in honey instead of salt. Salt is the best preserving medium, so unless you plan to eat the fish quickly, brine (salt water) is the best soaking medium.

Eels, mussels, bluefish, and trout are all outstanding smoked, but many other fish are surely as good; I just haven't had time to try them all. Smoked oysters are unbelievably good, but the raw materials are expensive. Generally, oily fishes are best for smoking, as the light taste of a delicate fish is overwhelmed by the smoky taste. Try some and see.

A properly constructed cement-block smokehouse gives the best consistent fish quality, but most of us are a bit less affluent. If you have the space and money, by all means build this kind of smoker—top quality is worth a lot. Your local library will have resources, or send a letter and I will help. For us po' folk, the choice boils down to the old refrigerator or one of several commercial models. For under $100 you can buy a charcoal or electric smoker that is generally acceptable, if not precisely controlled. The Brinkman, for example, gives a fast smoke to the fish compared to the Little Chief, which takes roughly four times as long. Long smoking at lower temperature (Little Chief) gives a much smoother-tasting product, but the slower smoker has no insulation, so it cannot maintain steady heat when the ambient temperature drops below about 50° F. I smoked a batch of bluefish for three days when ambient temperatures were around 50° F., but the fish was still not done. The insulated Country Smoke House works down to 0° F., but costs five times as much as simpler models.

CANNING

The long-term method of preserving fish, canning can be fatal if not done correctly. Its big advantage is illustrated by the three-year-old jar of tuna I opened the other day; the meat was just as good as the day it was canned.

The U.S. Department of Agriculture recommends processing pint jars of fish at a steam pressure of 10 pounds for 1 hour and 40 minutes so as to kill all bacteria. Obviously, you can't can fish without a pressure canner. But the method is so useful that I use it routinely for tuna (see page 159) and for other fish. Remeber, *do not deviate from the times and pressures given*. This is the one time when it is not safe to experiment.

FREEZING

The deep freeze is the best-known modern preservation method. It has one serious drawback: freezer burn. If you don't know what that is, you are singularly blessed. Briefly, freezer burn is a state of dehydration brought about by exposure to air and/or light, resulting in a product that is considerably less than optimum. Avoiding freezer burn remains the great challenge, but I have come up with some pretty effective measures, and their quirks:

1. *Glazing.* Dip each fillet in water, then lay it on a tray to freeze. After the fillet is frozen, dip it again and freeze it again. A third dip and freeze give pretty good insurance that the fish is well protected from the air. Now wrap the fillet in an opaque wrap (freezer paper is effective and much less expensive than aluminum foil). Mark the packages with the contents and date (it is frustrating to pull out a package and wonder what it contains), and store them in the deep freeze. Obviously, this is a long and tedious process—although the results are excellent.

2. *Cling wrap.* Wrap each fillet in cling wrap, then opaque wrap. Label and store as before. Sounds great? Make sure the cling wrap covers the meat tightly, otherwise the freezer will quickly burn the fillets. This is not a technique for long-term storage, as it is too easy to let air in to the meat.

3. *Milk-carton freezing.* Drop the fillets into a cleaned milk carton and fill the carton with water. Allow room for expansion—ice occupies considerably more space than the water it is formed from. (We discovered this on a winter camping trip in Vermont, years ago. We left a milk bottle full of water on the table at night and found a bottle-shaped ice cube surrounded by a pile of broken glass in the morning.) If the ice exapnds too much, modern pasteboard cartons will burst and expose your fish to the light. This method has its disadvantages, however. Is a quart of fillets what you want every time? And storage space is chopped up badly by these angular blocks of ice.

4. *Self-sealing plastic bags.* Place each meal-size portion in a self-sealing or zip-lock bag, evacuate the air, and seal. Then wrap the fish (marked, naturally) in

opaque freezer paper. There are vacuum package machines that, while expensive to own and operate, are said to give incredibly long storage life. Personally, I prefer to put water in each portion to cover the fish, then squeeze out most of it so that the fish is coated with water inside the bag. The additional storage life of this packaging method makes the effort worthwhile.

Since we store much fish by freezing, and since we're usually in a hurry for supper, I've developed quick ways to prepare frozen fillets. I drop chunks of frozen fish in a wire basket and steam them until they change appearance and flake apart.

DEHYDRATING

The advantages of dried fish are easily available with the modern dehydrator. Just load the fish fillets onto the shelf, turn on the power, and go about your business. I don't care much for dried fish, and the dryers I've seen so far process only a small amount (four or five pounds) at a time, but product quality is uniform and the fish keeps well as long as you keep it dry.

FISHELLANEOUS

O rganizing material into handy chapters based on fish care or type and lo-cation is fine, to a point. But some things don't fit well in this scheme. Pastries, batters, and some fish preparations, because of their breadth of application, require a chapter of their own. Here are some of these oddballs.

BASIC PASTRY

Makes enough for 1 large crust.

Great pastry is *not* difficult to make, but it is a painstaking enterprise. Too much flour toughens a pastry; too much water makes it soggy; too much shortening makes it greasy. My grandmother's recipe is given here. (Her pie crust was so well known that people drove as much as thirty miles by horse and buggy to buy her pies.) Her version uses lard. Goose fat makes probably the best pastry of all, whereas butter, oil, and margarine do *not*.

I N G R E D I E N T S

1 cup all-purpose flour

1/3 cup lard, at room temperature

Approximately 2 tablespoons ice water

P R O C E D U R E

Sift the flour three times into a bowl. Cut half the lard into the flour with a pair of knives or a pastry cutter. Do not mix, as this develops the gluten and makes the pastry tough. Cut the rest of the lard into the mix and work until approximately pea-size lumps form. Make a depression in the middle and sprinkle in a tablespoon of water. Mix with a fork; part of the dough will stick together. Sprinkle less remaining water than what you think will make the rest stick, then fork it some more. Careful; too much water makes it soggy. When the pastry can be formed into a ball, it is ready to chill. *Do not work the dough more than you have to or it will be tough.* Wrap the ball of dough in wax paper and chill it for 15 minutes.

Preheat oven to 350° F. Roll dough out on a floured pastry cloth to 1/8-inch thickness and use as directed in recipe. if using to line a pie pan, bake for 10 minutes, then remove crust from the oven and let cool before filling and baking further.

BEER BATTER

Do you have a favorite pancake recipe? If so, try substituting beer for the water or milk; dip fish pieces in this mixture and deep-fry them.

BASIC FISH BATTER

Makes enough to fry 2 pounds of fillets.

There are many good commercial fish-batter mixes, but this is my personal choice. For this recipe, beer is fine for mildly flavored fish, but strong-flavored fish such as mackerel can be cooked with sherry as part of the liquid. Strong flavors overpower a mild fish such as cod. Try fresh apple cider for bluefish cheeks.

I N G R E D I E N T S

1 cup flour (half all-purpose flour and half corn meal, whole wheat, or rice flour)
1 teaspoon baking powder
1–2 large eggs (2 eggs give crispier crust)
Liquid to make a fairly thin batter
Seasonings (optional)

P R O C E D U R E

Mix the flour, baking powder, and egg(s) in a large bowl. Slowly add the liquid while stirring. The thickness of the coating on the fish is determined by the amount of liquid: more liquid results in a thin batter which gives a thin coating, while less liquid gives a thicker batter resulting in a thicker, puffier fish crust. You may wish to add seasonings, such as garlic powder, paprika, or pepper. Instead of salt, which I don't think is especially healthful, I add a small amount of good sodium-free soy sauce.

DENNIS'S BATTER

Makes enough to coat 2 pounds of fillets.

This is the recipe a friend uses to make delicious deep-fried perch.

INGREDIENTS

1 cup all-purpose flour
2 large eggs
Approximately 1 cup milk

Seasoning salt, such as Mrs. Dash
Garlic powder
2 tablespoons dill pickle juice

PROCEDURE

Pat fish fillets dry with paper towels. Mix ingredients to form batter. Do not over-mix, as this develops the gluten in the flour and makes the finished coating tough. Adjust the thickness of the coating by varying the amount of milk; a thick batter gives a heavy coating.

MALTESE FISH DINNER

Serves 4

In this light meal, a clear fish broth with pasta or rice forms the entrée. The fish from the broth is served on a bed of grated carrots, accompanied by separate dishes of freshly ground black pepper, lemon juice, and parsley. A tossed salad with basil dressing is a frequent accompaniment, as is a simple potato salad.

INGREDIENTS

Fish, clean but left whole (type and quantity are whatever you have on hand)
Olive oil   1 medium onion, quartered

1 clove garlic

1 green pepper, quartered, cored, and
    seeded

1 celery stalk with leaves

Fresh mint leaves, or 1 bay leaf

Fresh basil leaves

1 small tomato, or 1 tablespoon tomato
    sauce

Peel of 1/2 lemon

1/2 pound of small-sized pasta or 1 cup
    of rice

2 large carrots

P R O C E D U R E

Fillet the fish and set the fillets aside, either for the main dish or for a later meal. Lightly oil the bottom of a large, heavy pot, and warm over medium heat. When hot, add the fillets, onion, garlic, green pepper, celery and leaves, mint leaves or bay leaf, basil, tomato, and the lemon peel. Sauté briefly, then add water to cover plus 1/2 inch, and boil gently for about 20 minutes. Add the fish head, tail, and skeleton. (The head is most important as it contains most of the flavor.) Boil for about 5 minutes, or until the fish is done, then strain the broth into another pot. Cook the rice or pasta until tender, then drain and add to the broth.

Grate the carrots and make a bed with them on a fish platter. Traditionally, the pieces of fish are carefully picked from the bones and placed on the carrot bed. Alternatively, you can prepare the fillets separately. Serve with pepper, lemon juice, and fresh parsley.

Basil dressing is made by combining olive oil, a fresh garlic clove, and a handful of fresh basil leaves in a blender or food processor. Blend until smooth. Serve with your favorite salad and sprinkle with a little grated Parmesan cheese for a real gourmet touch.

FISH TERRA-COTTA

Serves 2

D o you like flaky but moist fish, where each piece of meat stands out and savory vegetables add a special spark? If so, you'll probably like Fish Terra-Cotta. It is made with a covered terra-cotta baking dish with a handle on the end. You put the fish and vegetables inside and when you close the dish, the fish and vegetables are sealed inside to cook in their own juices. A tightly closed glass dish will work, but it does not give quite the same flavor.

I N G R E D I E N T S

- 1/4 cup chopped onion or 2 tablespoons chopped garlic
- 1 tablespoon margarine
- 1/2 pound of white fish fillets (bluefish, mackerel, and other oily fishes are not suited to this type of cooking.)
- 1/2 cup sliced fresh mushrooms
- 1/4 cup grated cheddar cheese (optional)
- 2 tablespoons dry sherry
- 1 cup chopped vegetables (broccoli, zucchini, cauliflower, Brussel sprouts)
- Large sprig of parsley

P R O C E D U R E

Place the onion or garlic and 1 teaspoon margarine in a microwave-safe dish and cook on high power for about 2 minutes, or until soft. You can also saute them. Lay the fish fillets in the terra-cotta dish. Cover with mushrooms and onion or garlic. Sprinkle with cheese. Lightly sprinkle with sherry and cover with vegetables. Close the dish and set it on a wood stove or in a slow oven (200–250° F.) for about 1 hour. Open the dish, being careful of escaping steam, and place the contents on individual plates, garnished with parsley.*

CRACKER-STYLE FISH

This recipe was given to us by a neighbor in Florida (his name for this method of cooking). We have since tried it on a variety of fish and found it outstanding, especially when the fish has a fairly strong flavor, such as the various snappers and porgies of southern waters.

25

* If you put foil wrapped garlic bread on the stove at the same time as the fish it will be ready at about the same time (on a wood stove, turn it frequently to avoid over-browning). Those who use modern heat for cooking will have to adjust the recipe themselves.

. . . .

Fish fillets

Butter

Half a Grapefruit

P R O C E D U R E
. . . .

Place the fillets on aluminum foil and bend up the edges of the foil to form walls so as to contain any liquid that develops. Dot the fish with butter and squeeze the juice of the grapefruit over the fish. Cover loosely with more aluminum foil. Place the dish on a hot outdoor grill and cook until the fish flakes apart. Indoor cooking is, of course, possible, but when you've spilled fish juice all over the oven, you'll understand why outdoors is preferable. The grapefruit juice, fish juice, and butter combine to make a marvelous sauce.

JERK-STYLE FISH

A fillet serves one

This is a Jamaican preparation for most fish and is memorably delicious. The spices are a closely guarded secret but you can purchase them at shops that stock Caribbean and South American groceries (the Fish House, Key Largo, FL, is my source.)

I N G R E D I E N T S
. . . .

Fish fillets

Margarine

Jerk spices

P R O C E D U R E
. . . .

Dot the fish with margarine and sprinkle with spices to taste. Broil until fish flakes. The resulting fish is rather spicy, a mixture of cardamom, three kinds of pepper, and ginger. Other ingredients remain a mystery. Corn on the cob seems to be the most popular accompaniment.

SMOKED FISH PIZZAETTES

Serves 4

Next time you feel like a pizza snack, try smoked mullet, bluefish, trout, or mackerel as toppings. Smoked fish on pizza is excellent.

INGREDIENTS

4 English Muffins

1 cup tomato sauce

1 cup grated cheese, your choice

1/2 cup smoked fish, chopped or flaked

PROCEDURE

Preheat oven to 400° F. Split English Muffins in half and place on a cookie sheet. Spread 1 to 2 tablespoons of the sauce on each half and sprinkle with cheese. Top with the fish. Bake until muffins are crispy and cheese bubbles, about 10 minutes.

T H R E E

CHOWDERS, SOUPS, AND SUCH

F ish soups of various types are made wherever fish can be had. The famous
French soup bouillabaisse uses safron and/or orange parts to balance the basic fish flavor, while American fish soups and chowders lean toward tomatoes or
milk. Gumbo, which is basically a stew, uses both tomatoes and okra to impart a
uniquely American character.

Although many types of non-fin fish are used in chowders, the most popular
are clams, scallops, mussels, shrimp, oysters, and, for the affluent, lobster.
Shrimp, scallops, and crabs are generally used sparingly in other fish soups to give
them extra character but are seldom a base for chowders. Conchs and whelks are

also used widely, but crabs generally do not have strong enough flavor for chowders and soups. Gumbo usually features shrimp, crabs, or prawns. Oysters and lobsters make delicious stews, while other shellfish are used mainly for chowders.

Most fish are adaptable to chowder or stew, but certain ones are especially so. My favorites are blackfish, cunners, pollock, cusk (yellow eel), cod, snapper, catfish, and yellow perch.

Gumbos are an invention from the Vieux Carré of New Orleans, where the regional cooking styles of French, Spanish, and African Ameroids blend to form one of the great world cuisines. A gumbo is essentially a stew of tomatoes and okra with various meats and/or fishes. A simple fare, gumbo doesn't sound very glamorous but it can be.

CLAM CHOWDERS—THE CONTROVERSY

There are basically four kinds of clam clowder: two with tomatoes, one with milk, and one with neither. The two tomato chowders are both sold under the label "Manhattan," but this is, to my mind, an insult to the exquisitely executed chowders of Rhode Island. In my years in and around Manhattan, *not once* did I encounter a chowder other than the standard heavily spiced version with either overcooked sea clams or whelks for meat. Rhode Island chowders—whether from the great cakes and chowder halls or locally brewed—have tender clams and delicate, if any, seasoning. The label "New England" is applied to creamy chowders, even though I doubt that more than 5 percent of the chowders made in New England contain milk. The true regional chowder of New England is thickened with potatoes cooked until they start to fall apart, which also gives a creamy appearance. However, since this chowder takes a long time to prepare, commercial interests have made a version that has very little to do with true New England chowder.

The other major debate about chowders regards onions. To use or not to use, that is the question. Celery raises no such furor. My personal preferences for chowder are as follows:

- Manhattan Chowder—Feed it to the neighborhood cats. (Please, don't poison my dog.)

- Rhode Island Chowder—A little onion, please. Usually excellent.

- Creamy New England Chowder—Perhaps one in eight is good, three may be edible, and occasionally one is very good. (I am referring to the creamy chowders, not true New England chowder.)

- Old-fashioned Chowder—Onion is optional, but the chowders are almost always excellent. This is the true New England chowder, not the mislabeled commercial product.

GRAM'S OLD-FASHIONED CLAM CHOWDER

Serves 4

Cold winter days brightened when she poured a piping hot ladle of this chowder over the pat of butter in my waiting bowl.

I N G R E D I E N T S

8–10 large quahogs
About 2 ounces lean salt pork (bacon is a fair substitute)
1 tablespoon vegetable oil (olive is best)

1 medium yellow onion, diced

4 medium potatoes, diced

1 tablespoon cooking oil (olive is best)

1–2 quarts of water

Salt, pepper, basil, tarragon to taste

P R O C E D U R E

Quahogs, the round hardshell clams, are frequently found in mud or sandy bottoms. Since Gram didn't care much for grit in her false teeth (it's not too pleasant in bridgework, either), she put her live clams in clean water overnight and then in cornmeal for 4 or 5 hours. The clams seemed to like this treatment since they cleaned themselves very efficiently; I never had grit in one of her chowders. While the clams steamed open in a big pot on the back of the wood stove, she diced the salt pork and rinsed it in fresh water to remove excess salt (I prefer boiling the pork for a minute or two to remove the salt). She then sautéed it in oil for about 5 minutes, stirring often until the pork was golden brown. (How tasty, those little bits of pork when no one was looking.) The onions then went into the pot to simmer until soft, while Gram diced the potatoes. By then the clams were open, so she added their broth with enough water to cover the ingredients. Salt, pepper, and basil went in, too, but the clam meat was held back. She added the potatoes and simmered the chowder until they softened. (The broth level was about 1/2 inch above the solid ingredients.) Meanwhile, she finely chopped the clam meats and added the clams in the last 5 minutes of cooking, after the potatoes had softened. Gram then served the chowder piping hot.

RHODE ISLAND
CLAM CHOWDER

Serves 4

Notice the lack of grease. This is the traditional Rhode Island chowder as prepared in the region's restaurants and chowder halls. For more tender clams, shuck them alive and cook the liquid along with the other ingredients, adding the chopped clams at the last minute or so. Fresh tomatoes are a pleasant replacement for the tomato sauce, but they extend the cooking time. Vary the quantities here to suit your taste. Add a small amount of dill weed or tarragon.*

I N G R E D I E N T S

6 quahogs
6 medium potatoes
1 medium onion
2 stalks celery
2 small cans (1 3/4-size) tomato sauce

P R O C E D U R E

Scrub the clams thoroughly with a brush under running fresh water to remove all grit and detritus.

Boil and dice the potatoes. Chop the onion and celery. Place the onion and celery in a 3- to 4-quart pot, half full of water, and bring to a boil. Add the clams to the hot water and remove as soon as they open. Reduce the liquid if it seems to be too much. Add the potatoes and tomato sauce, and stir over low heat. Meanwhile, chop the clams finely. Add clams just before serving.

MANHATTAN CHOWDER

Serves 4

Personally, I consider Manhattan clam chowder an affront to both chowder lovers and clams. The heavy use of herbs and vegetables hides the taste of the overcooked conchs or surf clams typically used. Unless you are fond of rubber tires in a spiced tomato sauce, don't bother. But if you really want to know how to make Manhattan chowder, try this.

*Tarragon and celery impart rather similar flavors to chowder, so keep the balance by backing off on one when you increase the other.

1/2 pound bacon or salt pork, diced

2 celery stalks

2 small onions

1/4 green bell pepper

1 large carrot

1–2 chili peppers to taste (optional)

4 medium tomatoes, chopped or 1 8-ounce can tomato sauce or 1 10-ounce can of condensed tomato soup

2 bay leaves

1 teaspoon dried thyme

1/4 teaspoon dried sage

2 cups clam juice

2 cups diced potatoes

2 cups chopped surf (skimmer) clams or conchs (whelks)

Salt and pepper to taste

P R O C E D U R E

Cook the bacon until fat is rendered. Save about half the drippings. Chop the celery, onions, green pepper, carrot, and chili peppers, then sauté in the bacon drippings. Add the tomatoes or sauce and continue cooking until the ingredients are tender, about 5 minutes. Add the herbs, clam juice, and chopped potatoes. Add enough water to cover the ingredients by 1/4 inch. Simmer until the potatoes are well cooked, about 30 minutes. Add the clams in the last minute of cooking, and season to taste.

NEW ENGLAND (CREAMY) CLAM CHOWDER

Serves 4

I N G R E D I E N T S

About 2 ounces lean salt pork or bacon

8–10 large quahogs, carefully washed

1 medium onion

1–2 teaspoons finely chopped green bell pepper

4 medium potatoes, diced

1 12-ounce can evaporated milk

1-1/2 cups whole or low-fat milk

Chopped fresh tarragon and/or pepper to taste (optional)

P R O C E D U R E

Slice the salt pork into thin strips. Place in a heavy 2-quart pot and cover with about 1/4 inch water. Bring the water to a boil and boil for 3 to 4 minutes. Open and chop the quahogs. Refrigerate the meat and juice separately. Pour the water off the pork and return the pot to the heat to brown the freshened pork thoroughly. Pour most of the pork drippings into the dog's dish, saving only enough to sauté the onion and green pepper. When the onion is transparent and the pepper is soft, about 3 minutes, add the potatoes and brown for a couple of minutes, stirring constantly (potatoes scorch easily, so keep stirring). Add the clam juice and enough water to cover the ingredients by 1/4 inch. Cover the pot and simmer, adding water as necessary, until the potatoes begin to disintegrate and the chowder appears milky. Add the milk. (Transfer the ingredients to a double boiler if you wish. This will reduce the risk of scorching the milk and adding an off flavor.) Season with tarragon and/or pepper, and simmer for 10 minutes or so, stirring constantly. Add the clam meat only at the last minute of cooking; do not overcook.

MUSSEL CHOWDER

Substitute mussels for clams in any of the clam chowder recipes. Do not use the mussel juice, however; it tends to be much saltier than that of clams and adding water will not relieve the saltiness, so discard the juice. Steam the mussels open and discard the byssal threads. Proceed as with clams. If you like, add a bottle of clam juice for flavor.

CAPTAIN'S CHOWDER

Serves 4

A great part of the pleasure of off-shore fishing on the *Yankee Captains Out O' Gloucester* is the chowder made with freshly caught fish. One cook (now retired, unfortunately) made such a great chowder that I practically begged him to share the recipe with us. On our last trip together he dictated this recipe to me. I hope you enjoy it as much as I have.

I N G R E D I E N T S

1 tablespoon vegetable oil, preferably olive

2 garlic cloves, chopped

1/4 cup finely diced lean salt pork

1 medium onion, finely chopped

1/4 medium green bell pepper, finely chopped

1 pimiento or 1/2 small tomato, finely diced

3 medium potatoes, boiled and diced

1–3 pounds boneless cooked fish (cusk, cod, haddock, or pollock)

1 6-ounce can evaporated milk

About 1-1/2 quarts milk

1 tablespoon butter or margarine (optional)

Salt and pepper

Chopped fresh basil or marjoram

P R O C E D U R E

Place oil in a large, deep iron or enameled pot and put pot over medium heat. Add garlic and sauté for approximately 3 minutes. Add salt pork and continue cooking for another 5 minutes or until the pork is golden brown. Pour off most of the drippings if you desire, but keeping them gives chowder better flavor. Add butter if you did not retain salt pork grease, and sauté the onion and green pepper until tender, about 5 minutes. Add the salt, pepper, and basil and stir. Then add the pimiento, potato, and fish. (I cook the fish by steaming it with a little water and

35

then add that water to the chowder). Finally, add the milks. Add enough liquid to cover the ingredients by 1/2 inch; add water if necessary. (An extra step worth taking is to transfer everything to a double boiler when adding the milk. This reduces the danger of scorching which can add an off flavor.) Heat through, *do not boil*. Season to taste.

RHODE ISLAND FISH CHOWDER

Serves 4

This is a mild chowder with neither oil nor milk.

INGREDIENTS

1 pound cod or other mild fish fillets
1 pound potatoes, peeled and diced
2 celery stalks, finely chopped
1 small onion, finely chopped

2 6-ounce cans tomato juice
1 teaspoon fresh dill or tarragon*
Pepper

PROCEDURE

Place fish in pan and add enough water to cover two-thirds thickness of the fillets. Bring to a boil, cover the pan, and remove from the heat. Let sit for 5 minutes. The fish will continue cooking until done. Reserve fish and broth. Precook the potatoes with the celery and onions until softened, about 10 minutes. Put the potato mix and fish in a large pot along with the reserved broth. Add enough water to cover by 1/4 inch, cover, and simmer for about 30 minutes. Blend in the tomato juice, tarragon or dill, and pepper. Mix well, cover, and simmer for another 30 minutes. Serve with crisp oyster crackers.

36

*If you use celery, cut down on the tarragon, as they give similar flavors to a soup.

CUNNER CHOWDER

. . . .

The cunner (bergal, blue perch, or ocean perch) is especially good in a Rhode Island fish chowder recipe. Don't cover the pot in cooking, however; these fish foam incredibly, as I found by nearly blowing up the kitchen with a pressure cooker.

BLUEFISH CHOWDER

. . . .

Bluefish (if properly bled, iced, and dark meat removed) can make a very good chowder. First microwave the meat and discard the resulting juice to eliminate most of the strong flavor. Then follow your favorite chowder recipe.

SNAPPER CHOWDER

. . . .

Snappers (red, mutton, mangrove, yellowtail, vermillion, etc.) are excellent in chowder, especially after having been frozen. I brought about fifty quarts of snapper fillets back to New England from the Florida Keys. Quite by accident, I found that Captain's Chowder (page 35) made with frozen snapper fillets was even better than when made with the customary fresh fish. The warm-water fish seems to impart more flavor to the soup.

CONCH CHOWDER

Serves 3

Conchs (or whelks) are very large and very tough saltwater snails. Conch meat for chowder is normally acquired by breaking off the large end of the shell of the gastropod (literally, "stomach-foot"). This breaks its anchorage and it can then be pulled from its shell and eviscerated for cooking. Chop and put the cleaned meat through a grinder. Then, as with clams, add the meat to the chowder in the last moments of cooking.

INGREDIENTS

1 large conch or several small
1–2 ounces salt pork, cut in 1/4-inch-
    wide strips; or 3–5 strips of bacon
2 celery stalks
1 large onion
1/4 green bell pepper
3 medium potatoes

2 cups clam juice
1 bay leaf
1 teaspoon dried thyme
1 teaspoon dried sage
Pepper
2 8-ounce cans tomato juice

PROCEDURE

Cut the dark meat from the conch and discard. Cut the light meat into small pieces and set aside. Put the salt pork in a chowder pot and cover with water, boil to freshen, and discard the water. Return the salt pork to the heat and render it, saving approximately 1 teaspoon of drippings. Finely chop the celery, onion, and green pepper. Add these to the salt pork and sauté until tender, about 5 minutes. Peel and dice the potatoes and add to the vegetables. Stir in clam juice and enough water to cover the potatoes by 1/4 inch. Add the herbs and spices. Cover the pot and simmer until the potatoes are soft, about 10 minutes. Add tomato juice and simmer for another 20 minutes. Add the minced conch meat in the last couple minutes of cooking.

CATFISH GUMBO

Serves 4 to 6

Serve this over rice with a side order of cornbread. Many people like to add hot sauce to their gumbo; I would advise caution at first. Although this nominally serves 4 to 6 people, don't accept this as a hard-and-fast measure. Proportions in this dish are highly variable, very much a matter of individual taste.

I N G R E D I E N T S

3–5 *slices bacon*
1/2 *cup chopped onion*
1 *cup sliced okra*
3 *cups peeled and chopped fresh tomatoes*
About 3 pounds cleaned and skinned catfish

P R O C E D U R E

Fry the bacon until crisp in a large, deep iron pan, about 10 minutes. Set the bacon aside on brown paper or paper towels to drain. Sauté the onion in bacon fat until soft, about 3 minutes, then add the okra and sauté until half done, about 3 minutes. Then add the tomatoes and simmer over medium heat for about 20 minutes, until the ingredients blend well. While the tomato mix is simmering, steam the catfish until the meat falls off the bones. Add the catfish meat to the gumbo and cook only enough to blend the ingredients.

SHRIMP GUMBO

Serves 4 to 6

This classic from the South uses crab meat and oysters to make a dish that is fabled in song.

. . . .

1/2 cup chopped onion

1 tablespoon butter

2 tablespoons all-purpose flour

1-1/2 cups strained tomatoes, preferably fresh

4 cups fish, chicken, or beef stock

4 cups thin-sliced okra

1/2 pound peeled and deveined shrimp

1/2 pound crab meat

16 medium shucked oysters

Fresh parsley

P R O C E D U R E
. . . .

Soften the onions in butter for about 2 minutes in a microwave oven. Transfer to deep, heavy kettle and stir in the flour. Simmer over low heat for about 30 minutes, stirring constantly, to make a brown roux (paste of flour and butter). Stir in the tomatoes and stock, blending with a wire whisk until smooth. Add okra, while constantly stirring for about 5 minutes. Add the shrimp and crab and simmer until the okra is tender, about 10 minutes. Add the oysters. The gumbo is done when the oysters are plump and curled, about 1 minute. Garnish individual servings with parsley.

OYSTER STEW

Serves 2

This is not a low-cholesterol dish. My step-father's father made this stew every Friday night for as long as I knew him.

I N G R E D I E N T S
. . . .

1 quart milk

1 cup light cream

4 tablespoons (1/2 stick) butter

1 cup shucked oysters, with liquor

Pepper

Paprika (optional)

Combine milk, cream, butter, and oyster liquor in the top of a double boiler. Cook 20 to 30 minutes over boiling water, then add oysters and pepper. Garnish with paprika. Cook just until oysters are firm, about 1 minute.

LOBSTER STEW

A popular song has touted the taste of "lobster stew, served by a window with an ocean view." I never figured out who was doing the serving, but apparently Cape Cod received a lot of publicity for this dish. The only way I know to make the dish is to steam a live lobster and add the juice and tomalley (the green stuff you find when you open the lobster's body cavity) to the milk, cream, and butter in Oyster Stew (previous recipe). Clean the meat from the shell and add it to the liquids shortly before serving.

CATFISH STEW

Serves 4 to 6

I N G R E D I E N T S

3–5 catfish
4 medium potatoes, finely chopped
1–2 medium onions, finely chopped
2 celery stalks, finely chopped

41

Eviscerate and skin the catfish. Place the fish in a steamer and steam until the flesh falls off the bones. Discard the bones and separate the fish and juice. Place potatoes, onions, and celery in a large pot. Add the fish juice and enough additional water to cover. Cook until the vegetables are tender, about 5 minutes, then add the reserved fish meat. Simmer to blend the flavors, about 10 to 15 minutes.

YELLOW PERCH STEW

Serves 4

Codlike fish work well in this soup, as do cusk and other mild fishes.

I N G R E D I E N T S

- 1–2 tablespoons salt pork
- 1 celery stalk, finely chopped
- 1 small onion, minced
- 3–4 medium potatoes, diced
- 1–3 pounds perch fillets

- 2 medium tomatoes, peeled and finely chopped
- Garlic powder
- Tamari
- Tabasco sauce

P R O C E D U R E

Cut salt pork into approximately 1/4-inch thick strips and put in a large pot with water to cover. Bring to a boil. (Boiling draws the salt from the pork and freshens it.) Boil for 3 minutes, then discard the water. Rinse the pork and return it to the pot and brown it, about 3 minutes. Discard most of the pork drippings. While the pork is browning, boil the celery and onion in one pot and the potatoes in another, until tender but firm—3 minutes for the celery and 8 minutes for potatoes. Drain onion and celery and mix them with the salt pork in the pot. Put the perch fillets in pot with the potatoes. Add tomatoes to pot with onion and celery and cook for 5 minutes. Add potatoes and fish to the vegetables, stir, and add enough water to give a chowder consistency (liquid should be about 1/2 inch above solid ingredients). Season to taste with garlic powder, tamari, and a drop of Tabasco sauce. To fully develop the flavor of the soup, simmer it for several hours (e.g. on a wood stove).

FINLESS

FISH

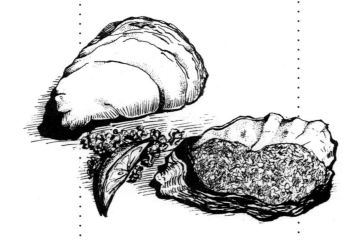

F O U R
. . . .

CLAMS

. . . .
There are many varieties and styles of preparation for clams. For example, the quahog (*Merceneria merceneria*)* is a different eating proposition in Maine than in Florida—the flesh of this round clam is quite differently flavored in the two regions. All that we have tried are good eating, but cold-water clams are quite good raw.†

Likewise, there are many ways to open a clam. Gulls use gravity and large rocks, but this tends to put pieces of clam shell and sand in the meat. People of the BFS

---

* The biologist who named these clams must have had at least a minimum of sense of humor. The translation of the Latin name is literally "Money money." He observed the Indian tribes using the shell of this clam as their "wampum" or medium of exchange and created this imaginative nomenclature.

† Caution: *Don't ever use dead clams or clams from suspected contaminated waters.* Dead clams are deadly; contaminated clams, an invitation to hepatitis. Live clams are tightly closed.

(brute force and stupidity) school are easily identified by the scars on their hands. The steam'em shuckers are easily identified by extreme molar development. Affluent shuckers have been known to invest in a mechanical variety of shucker (a gadget that looks and works much like a miniature guillotine). If you prize cherrystone clams (raw on the half-shell), then such a mechanical gadget can be worthwhile. The quahog can be opened by inserting the tip of a clam knife at the umbo (hinge) of the clam and wiggling it open. The simplest method is to freeze the live animal and thaw it when ready to open; it is then very easy to get a clam knife between the valves (shell halves) and cut the adductor muscles (muscles which hold the shell halves closed). Save the juice for chowder and chop the meats to make whatever dish you desire.

There are basically two types of clam: hard-shell and soft-shell. The soft-shell clams are easy to open and are good for "steamers." Hard-shell animals are excellent for most other purposes.

CLAMS CASINO

Serves 4

I N G R E D I E N T S

12 hard-shell clams

1 small onion, minced

1-1/2–2 cups seasoned bread crumbs

1/2 pound bacon strips

P R O C E D U R E

Preheat the broiler. Open the clams, chop the meats, and set aside the shells. Add minced onion to the clams to taste. Mix with bread crumbs and stuff the half-shells with the mix. Lay pieces of bacon over each stuffed shell. Assemble trays of stuffed clams and broil until the bacon is crisp, about 2 minutes. A dozen clams will usually serve me and my wife. Vary the quantities of ingredients to suit you, there's lots of room to play.

Note: When you fix these for a picnic or party, make at least twice what you think you will need. I've used bushels of clams at even relatively small parties. People snaffle these up like you wouldn't believe.

BAKED STUFFED CLAMS

Serves 4

I N G R E D I E N T S

24 quahogs

About 1/2 cup dry bread crumbs

1 small onion

2 garlic cloves

Fresh chopped herbs (parsley, basil,
    tarragon, dill)

4 tablespoons (1/2 stick) butter or
    margarine

Lemon juice (optional)

Paprika

P R O C E D U R E

Preheat the oven to 350° F. Open the clams and save the juice for chowder; reserve shells. Chop the clam meat and mix with the bread crumbs. Mince onion and garlic and add. Chop herbs and add. Melt butter and add to mix. Stir until fairly moist; if it is too dry, add some clam juice and/or lemon juice to moisten.*

Fill the half-shells, mounding the stuffing on top. Sprinkle with paprika and bake 15 minutes.

Note: Uncooked stuffed clams will keep for months in the freezer. Just cover them with plastic wrap or put in sealable plastic bags.

* You'll have to play with mix to get a feeling for the right consistency for stuffing. Quantities to achieve a desirable texture vary — depending, for instance, on how dry the crumbs are. A rough rule is crumbs from 6 slices of toast to 4 tablespoons of butter.

FRIED CLAMS

Serves 2

Generally, soft-shell clams are used for frying. A certain chain of restaurants along the Atlantic Coast is quite famous for its fried clams. I won't mention the name of the chain since it probably wouldn't like it revealed that it uses surf clam strips (what we use for bait in deep-sea fishing). Razor clams (so-called because the shell looks like an old-fashioned straight razor) are probably even tastier, but they are the hardest clam to dig and are, consequently, not commercially available. Any other clam is also suitable, but most others have other uses that preclude their adoption to frying.

I N G R E D I E N T S

Vegetable oil for deep-frying
2 pints clams strips or pieces person
1 cup batter of choice (pages 22–23)

P R O C E D U R E

Heat oil to 375° F. Make sure the cooking oil is thoroughly hot so clams will not absorb excessively. Dip the clams in batter and fry in hot oil for 30 seconds. Drain on paper towels. Serve with tartar sauce or ketchup.

STEAMED CLAMS

Any of the soft-shell clams is fine for this recipe. Put 1/4 inch of water in a steamer and heat. Wash the clams, put them in the steamer basket, and place in the steamer. Put a lid on and steam until the clams open. Lift clams out and take meats from the shells.

To serve, dip the meats in the liquid from steaming, then in melted butter (a teaspoon of lemon juice or a couple lemon verbena leaves to a 1/2 stick of butter adds a bit of zip). Some clams have skin on the neck that should be removed before eating, as it is rather tough.

CLAMS ON THE HALF-SHELL

Makes about 1 cup of sauce, or enough for 2 to 3 dozen clams

Inspect the live clams to make sure all are tightly closed. Discard any that are not. Scrub the shells with running water and a brush to remove any sand or mud. Open the clams by whatever method you prefer (see page 7) and serve them on the half-shell with the following Half-Shell Sauce or your favorite sauce. Use about 1/2 teaspoon sauce for each half-shell.

INGREDIENTS

1/4 cup prepared horseradish
1/4 cup ketchup
1/4 cup pickle relish
Tabasco sauce

Worcestershire sauce
Lemon juice to taste
2 tablespoons mayonnaise or salad dressing
2 tablespoons Dijon mustard (optional)

PROCEDURE

To horseradish, ketchup, and relish, add dashes of Tabasco sauce, Worcestershire sauce, and lemon juice to taste. Stir in mayonnaise and mustard and mix well. Adjust to taste—some people like much hotter sauce than others.

CLAM FRITTERS

Clam fritters are basically the same as fried clams except that much less liquid is used in the mixture, and the clams are very finely chopped. The clams and dry ingredients are mixed together in a bowl and moistened with just enough clam juice to make a thick batter. The thick batter is dropped into very hot oil by the teaspoonful and fried until crusty little balls form. When the balls are brown (takes only a few seconds), drain them on paper towels or brown paper bags.

Note: Traditionally, these clam cakes are served with chowder. Two great chowder halls existed in Rhode Island when I was growing up, but only the *Rocky Point* hall survives today. In these famous seafood restaurants it was all the clam cakes and chowder you could eat for a certain price. Regrettably, the chowder hall tradition is dying out.

TRADITIONAL CLAM BAKE

Yes, you do have clams at a clam bake, but the name of this famous festival is somewhat misleading. Lobsters, crabs, mussels, shrimp, clams, whole fish—virtually anything you can catch from the sea—as well as ears of corn in their husks are all more than acceptable. Tradition has it that the settlers copied this banquet from the coastal Indians. In any event, it's spectacular eating.

P R O C E D U R E

Dig a pit about 2 feet deep by the shore (or wherever you can get all the ingredients you'll need) and line it with rocks (don't use flat rocks from a streambed; they will explode). Build a hot hardwood fire in the pit. While the rocks are heating, gather lots of fresh seaweed and your food. Sweep the hot coals and ash out of the pit and put in a layer of wet seaweed, then the shellfish, fish, and corn, and add another layer of wet seaweed, quite thick this time. Cover the seaweed with a large piece of canvas and bury it with sand. Go play a game of softball, have a couple of beers, or do whatever else for about 3 to 4 hours. Come back and shake the sand off the canvas (canvas keeps the sand out of your food), dig off the top layer of seaweed, and dig into some succulent eating. Melted butter and/or lemon juice go extremely well as garnishes.

WHITE CLAM SAUCE FOR PASTA

A classic of Italian cuisine.

INGREDIENTS

Clams
Olive oil
Garlic, minced
Chopped fresh parsley
Cooked pasta
Grated Parmesan cheese

PROCEDURE

Open the clams by whatever method you prefer (see page 7). Chop the meats if they are large. Now pour a generous amount of olive oil into a cold frying pan and add the garlic. The oil is the bulk of the sauce, so figure accordingly; the amount of garlic is strictly chef's choice. Sauté the garlic for 1 to 2 minutes, then add the parsley and continue to sauté for 2 minutes more. Add the clams when the garlic is almost golden, and cook only for the few seconds necessary to make the garlic golden, not dark and bitter. Pour the sauce over the pasta, and add just a touch of cheese if desired. Serve with garlic bread.

BETTY'S CLAM DIP

Makes around 1 cup of dip

This is a quick and delicious party dip. The effort is minimum, but the compliments are not. My Aunt Betty taught me this one over thirty years ago and it remains one of my favorites.

INGREDIENTS

3–6 medium quahogs
1 8-ounce package cream cheese, at room temperature
Crudités: celery and carrot sticks, broccoli and cauliflower florets
Half-slices of cocktail rye or pumpernickel bread, potato chips and/or thin crackers.

PROCEDURE

Open the clams and save juice. Chop the meats finely. Mix the clams, clam juice, and cream cheese in a serving bowl. Set the bowl in crushed ice on a serving platter, surrounded with crudités, bread, and crackers.

Note: Keep the bowl cool, as seafood spoils at room temperature.

MUSSELS

There are two kinds of mussels native to New England waters, the ribbed (or swamp) mussel and the blue (or edible) mussel. The ribbed mussel is greenish and has little ribs radiating out on its shell; it is generally considered too tough to eat by other than Swamp Yankees. I like them. The blue mussel has a smooth blue shell and delicate succulent flesh—when it is not overcooked. Both mussels occur in beds in shallow tidal waters, but I have also caught enormous blues in several hundred feet of water jig-fishing for codfish off Cashes Ledge, a series of underwater hills halfway between Nova Scotia and Gloucester, Massachusetts.

The reproductive method of these bivalves is an important thing to know, since it directly affects culinary preparation. Adults release their tiny "babies" into the water. These float free until they settle into a promising new home. When the young settle to the bottom of the sea (or on a wreck or piling), they put out strong roots (called byssal threads or beards) to anchor themselves for their adult lives. These threads, which mark the difference between mussels and the other bivalves, must be removed before you eat mussels.

An extremely important consideration with any bivalve is that *they are not contaminated*. Contaminated bivalves will only make you very sick, if you are lucky. Take mussels only where they are washed by clean ocean waters. If you have doubts about an area, ask a native or err on the side of caution and don't take the shellfish. Also, be sure that the shells of the animals you do take are tightly closed; an open shell contains a sick or dead creature.

STEAMED MUSSELS

Serves 2

INGREDIENTS

3–6 dozen mussels

2 cups water or wine

4 tablespoons (1/2 stick) butter

Chopped fresh herbs (tarragon, dill), minced garlic, or lemon juice (optional)

PROCEDURE

I prefer to scrub residual detritus off the shell before cooking. A vegetable brush and cool running water are all that are needed. Discard any opened mussels. Put the remainder in some kind of steamer, such as a perforated enameled pot nested inside a larger enameled pot. Add water or wine, and steam until mussels open.

While the mussels steam, melt the butter. Add herbs, garlic, and lemon if desired.

Remove mussels from the steamer and let cool enough to handle. Discard any unopened shells. Remove the byssal threads by pulling them loose from the meats. (As you process the meats, you may want to put them back in the steaming broth to keep them warm until you are ready.)

To serve, dip the meats in the melted butter and pop them in your mouth.

Note: In Europe and some parts of the United States, these tasty bivalves are raised in commercial beds. It is hard to believe that most Americans turn up their noses at such delicious food.

SMOKED MUSSELS

The broth obtained when you steam mussels is quite salty—just right, in fact, to serve as a marinating solution for smoking any leftover steamed mussels. Simply leave the steamed mussel meats in the broth for a couple of hours, depending on how salty you like your smoked mussels. Add a little dry sherry to the marinade for a nice touch.

Take the meats from the solution and spread them on a stainless-steel wire screen with mesh small enough to hold meats that will shrink to half the size of the originals.

Use green or wetted maple chips in your smoker. The smoking time varies depending on the particular smoker and the size of the load. My smoker gives a nice flavor to 4 or 5 pounds of steamed meats in about 25 minutes. For an interesting and unusual party hors d'oeuvre, try spreading cream cheese on sesame crackers and topping them with your own home-smoked mussels.

OYSTERS

Surely the ancient Greeks and Romans had a sense of humor, but just as surely their oyster gags have not survived. (Perhaps it's the historians who have
no sense of humor.) But there certainly is an abundance of oyster jokes today,
ranging from their resemblence to various bodily secretions to their supposed
aphrodisiac property. Fine. The less demand there is for oysters, the more there
are for me.

Oysters can be prepared in a variety of ways. But for the purist there is only one
acceptable way—raw, with an optional drop of hot sauce or horseradish. I normally don't bother with the optionals, especially if the shellfish come from certain offshore islands of New England. A few of the popular applications follow.

OYSTER STUFFING

INGREDIENTS

Your favorite stuffing base

Oysters, shucked and chopped

Duck, turkey, or other moderate to strongly flavored bird

PROCEDURE

Put stuffing in a large bowl and add oysters. Use to stuff bird and roast according to your favorite recipe.

Note: Because oysters have a very strong flavor when they are cooked, they must be used sparingly and with foods that can support this flavor. Wild duck or turkey, in particular, lend themselves to oyster stuffing. A stuffing of wild rice, mushrooms, chestnuts, and oysters makes a lovely complement to wild duck.

SMOKED OYSTERS

INGREDIENTS

Oysters

4 quarts water

1/2 cup nonidodized salt

PROCEDURE

Remove the oysters from the shell. Use the back end of an old-fashioned bottle opener to pry the shells apart. Put the rounded end of the opener in the umbo and twist—this will pop the oyster open. Soak the oysters in a moderate salt water solution for about 30 minutes. Freshen the meat by rinsing with cold water. Spread the oysters on a tight stainless-steel wire mesh that fits in the smoker. Put the oysters in the smoker and smoke with apple, hickory, or mesquite chips until solid. This time will vary depending on the particular smoker but varies from 2 to 10 hours. A hot smoker, such as the Brinkman, smokes quickly, while a cooler smoker, such as the Little Chief, gives much better control of the final product.

OYSTERS ROCKEFELLER

Serves 4 as an appetizer

I N G R E D I E N T S

1/2 cup spinach

2 tablespoons (1/4 stick) butter or margarine

2 teaspoons lemon juice

4 tablespoons chopped fresh parsley

1 dozen oysters, shucked and with shells retained

1 teaspoon onion juice

2 tablespoons cooked and minced bacon

P R O C E D U R E

Preheat the oven to 350° F. Puree spinach with butter, lemon juice, and parsley (a food processor is invaluable here) until smooth. Fill 12 half-shells with stuffing and put an oyster on top of each. Sprinkle with onion juice and bacon, and bake for about 10 minutes. Then run oysters under broiler to brown. Serve at once.

Note: Copy the New Orleans idea of sprinkling on a few drops of absinthe or a little grated Parmesan cheese before baking.

SCALLOPS

V enus is pictured rising from the sea on half a scallop shell. That should be
enough history on scallops. Here are a few ideas.

CREAMED SHRIMP AND SCALLOPS IN PASTRY SHELLS

Serves 3

I N G R E D I E N T S

Basic pastry dough (page 21)

1-1/2 cups chopped shrimp

1-1/2 cups chopped scallops

1 small onion, chopped and softened by cooking in microwave for 2 minutes

10-ounce can condensed cream of mushroom soup

A dash of dry sherry

Chopped fresh dill, tarragon, or garlic (optional)

8 sprigs parsley, for garnish

24 thin tomato slices

P R O C E D U R E

Preheat oven to 350° F. Make pastry shells by lining 8 greased muffin cups with pastry. Bake for 10 minutes or until the shells are lightly browned. Let cool on a rack. Lower oven temperature to 250° F.

Lightly steam the shrimp and scallops until cooked (I like to microwave them together for 5 minutes.) Save the juices. You can add softened chopped onions to the juices but be careful not to overdo it. Place shrimp, scallops, onion, and reserved juices in a bowl. Add the soup, sherry, and herbs and mix. Spoon the mix into the pastry shells and warm in the oven for about 15 minutes. To serve, garnish with parsley and surround with tomato slices.

SIMPLE SCALLOPS FOR TWO

Serves 2

I N G R E D I E N T S

4 thick slices bacon

1 pound bay scallops

1/2–3/4 cup fine seasoned bread crumbs

Slowly fry the bacon in a large cast-iron skillet until crisp, about 10 miniutes. Drain and use the bacon for another recipe. Wash the scallops in cold running water, put them on a plate and then roll in bread crumbs. Sauté the scallops slowly in the bacon fat until the largest has turned white inside (cut it open to see), about 2 minutes. *Don't overcook these little jewels; they are even good raw.*

SCALLOP-STUFFED MUSHROOMS

Serves 2

L iving where we do, around the corner from a mushroom plant, we find large mushrooms easily accessible. You may have more trouble locating them, but this dish is worth the effort.

I N G R E D I E N T S

8 large (3-inch diameter or better) fresh mushrooms

6 dinner rolls, broken apart

1/2 cup (1 stick) butter

1/2 pound bay scallops

Swiss cheese, sliced thin (optional)

Fresh parsley, for garnish

P R O C E D U R E

Preheat the oven to 350° F. Break the stems from the mushrooms. Chop the stems, the rolls, and the scallops until very fine. Mix these in a large bowl, then pour in melted butter and mix thoroughly. Stuff the mushroom caps with this mixture, then place the caps in a shallow baking dish. You may add a small piece of cheese to each mushroom cap, but avoid too much as the flavors are delicate. Bake for 20 minutes, then remove and garnish with parsley.

Note: This high-cholesterol dish can be made a little less so by substituting corn oil for the butter.

SCALLOP PIE

Serves 2 or 3

There are at least as many seasonings for this as there are pie makers. Oregano, basil, marjoram, and chili powder are popular warm-toned additives. Lemon juice, lemon verbena, and lemon balm are piquant, while Dijon mustard, horseradish, garlic, or cayenne give authority. Exotic touches range from cardamom to turmeric. Experiment, but gently. I like to add about 1/2 teaspoon of sherry, a light touch of chili powder, and a couple tablespoons of crumpled dried lemon balm leaves.

Traditionally, this pie is served with buttered asparagus tips and boiled small whole potatoes.

INGREDIENTS

1-1/2 pints finely chopped scallops
1/2 pound cooked and flaked codfish
1/2 cup cracker crumbs
1/4 teaspoon Worcestershire or soy sauce
1 large egg, beaten
1 cup milk
1 tablespoon butter, melted
Pepper, to taste
8-inch Basic Pastry shell and pastry for top crust (page 21)

PROCEDURE

Preheat the oven to 350° F. Combine scallops and codfish in a large bowl. Blend in the remaining ingredients and pour into the prepared crust. Cover with top crust and vent (fork holes). Bake for about 1 hour, or until crust is lightly browned.

Note: You may substitute monkfish or wolffish for the cod; these fish eat mostly lobsters and crabs, and their flavor reflects this.

POACHED SCALLOPS

Serves 2

1 tablespoon olive oil
Pinch of dry mustard
1 tablespoon soy sauce
1 tablespoon maple syrup

1 cup water
1/2 cup + 1 tablespoon dry sherry
3/4 pound scallops
1 tablespoon cornstarch

P R O C E D U R E

Heat a heavy, deep skillet and add the oil along with the mustard. Add soy sauce, maple syrup, water, and 1/2 cup of sherry. Bring these to a boil over medium heat, then lower the heat and simmer for about 5 minutes. Add the scallops and poach until done, about 2 minutes (the flesh is firm and white). Remove scallops to a warm platter. Dissolve the cornstarch in the 1 tablespoon sherry. Add to the poaching liquid and cook until reduced to a sauce, stirring constantly with a wire whisk to avoid lumps. Pour the sauce over the scallops and serve over rice or toast.

63

SCALLOPS

BROILED SCALLOPS

Serves 2

This is probably the simplest, yet one of the best, ways to prepare scallops.

INGREDIENTS

2–3 tablespoons butter or margarine
1 teaspoon chopped fresh herbs (tarragon, dill, basil, lemon balm)
Garlic (optional)
3/4 pound scallops

PROCEDURE

Preheat the broiler. Melt the butter and stir in herbs. Place scallops in a broiling dish and pour the butter over. Broil until the scallops are done (the flesh inside turns white), about 2 minutes.

BAKED SCALLOPS

Serves 2

Another very simple but good preparation for scallops.

INGREDIENTS

3/4 pound scallops   2–3 tablespoons butter, melted
1/2 cup seasoned bread crumbs

PROCEDURE

Preheat the oven to 350° F. Roll the scallops in seasoned bread crumbs, put in a baking dish, sprinkle with melted butter, and bake for approximately 15 minutes, depending on size. Good with rolls and French-style green beans.

DEEP-FRIED SCALLOPS

Serves 2

Deep-fried scallops are delicious but not recommended as a frequent visitor because of all the cholesterol (at least that is what my doctor says).

I N G R E D I E N T S

Vegetable oil for deep-frying
3/4 pound scallops
Fish batter (pages 22–23) or commercial mix

P R O C E D U R E

Heat the oil to at least 400° F. Dip the scallops in the batter and drop individually into the hot cooking oil. When the crusts are nicely browned, the scallops are done. My little sister uses ketchup with deep-fried shellfish, but I prefer to serve these with Louisiana red sauce, cocktail sauce, tartar sauce, or just lemon juice. A large green salad and fresh bread will help offset the oil.

STEAMED SCALLOPS

Put 1/4 inch of water in a steamer and place on the stove to heat. Put the scallops in a steamer basket and, when the water is boiling, lower the basket into the steamer and cover. Scallops are ready when the meat is solid and white, about 2 minutes. Lift them out and dip the meats in lemon butter, or simply in the juice in which they were steamed. The steaming juice can be saved as a base for chowder.

Note: While it is possible to steam these delicate mollusks, it is not the best preparation.

SHRIMP

Like scallops and oysters, much of the culinary history of shrimp is lost in antiquity. Here are a few favorite recipes.

SHRIMP COCKTAIL

Shrimp cocktail is boiled shrimp on ice, surrounded by lettuce, and accompanied by a Louisiana Red Sauce. The first time I ever tried a shrimp cocktail I was in my freshman year of college, my first time away from home. The sauce came from a jar. Nobody told me you are supposed to cook the shrimp before you make shrimp cocktail. My unfortunate roommate was a gentleman. He said, "This is very good, but . . . some people think it's even better when the shrimp are cooked."

I N G R E D I E N T S

1 package shrimp & crab boil
3–4 peeled and deveined shrimp per person
Crushed ice
Lettuce leaves
Louisiana Red Sauce (recipe follows) or commercial cocktail sauce

P R O C E D U R E

Stir the boil into a pot of boiling water, add the shrimp, and cook until red, 1–2 minutes. Remove the shrimp and chill in the refrigerator. Fill the serving dishes with crushed ice, put lettuce leaves around the perimeter of the dishes, and spread the cooled shrimp on top of the ice. Serve the sauce in a separate dish, as your guests may have slightly different tastes. Shrimp cocktail is usually accompanied by crackers or thin toast pieces.

LOUISIANA RED SAUCE (COCKTAIL SAUCE)

Makes 1 cup

I N G R E D I E N T S

1/4 cup prepared horseradish

1/4 cup ketchup

1/4 cup mustard

2 tablespoons mayonnaise

Dash of Worcestershire sauce

Dash of lemon juice

Dash of Tabasco sauce

1/4 cup relish (optional)

P R O C E D U R E

Mix horseradish, ketchup, mustard, and mayonnaise in a bowl. Add the Worcestershire, lemon, and Tabasco; you'll have to judge how much of each by experience—there is no rule other than taste to go by. Some people like to add relish to the sauce, but again, it's a personal matter. Only practice and experiment will give you the taste that satisfies.

BAKED STUFFED SHRIMP

Serves 1

This is probably one of the most famous shrimp dishes. The problem is expense. The very large (10 to 12 count per pound) shrimp are the most expensive.

I N G R E D I E N T S

2–3 jumbo or very large shrimp

About 1/4 pound finely chopped scallops

1/2 cup finely crushed crackers or bread crumbs

1/2 teaspoon tarragon (fresh or dried)

1/8 teaspoon fresh dill weed

2-1/2 tablespoons butter

1/2 garlic clove

About 1 tablespoon lemon or lime juice

P R O C E D U R E

Preheat the oven to 350° F. Clean and butterfly the shrimp. (Cut lengthwise from the back or vein side almost through and spread to look like a butterfly.) Place the butterflied shrimp on a baking dish. Mix crackers, herbs, and scallops in a mixing bowl. Melt butter in a skillet and sauté garlic until well browned, about 1 minute. Discard the garlic and add the lemon juice. Mix. Stir the lemon butter into the cracker mix. The stuffing should now stick together, but if not quite damp enough add a little extra lemon butter. Mound the stuffing on the shrimp and bake 3 to 5 minutes until stuffing is lightly browned. Don't overcook shrimp unless you are particularly partial to rubber.

SHRIMP SCAMPI

Serves 3

This dish is either broiled or pan-fried.

I N G R E D I E N T S

1/4 cup olive oil

2 tablespoons lemon juice

1 garlic clove, minced

1 pound peeled and deveined shrimp (leave tails on)

2 tablespoons chopped fresh parsley

69

Soften the garlic by microwaving with a tablespoon of olive oil for 1 to 2 minutes. In a large bowl mix garlic, olive oil, and lemon juice. Add shrimp and stir gently until completely coated. To broil, arrange shrimp in a single layer in a broil pan, pour the remaining juice over, and broil 6 to 8 minutes or until shrimp are tender. To pan-fry, put the oil mixture in the pan and sauté the shrimp until browned, about 2 minutes. Add the parsley and mix gently. The tails make handy handles for eating. Garlic bread and snow peas are amiable accompaniments.

SHRIMP NEWBURG

Serves 3 to 4

A Newburg sauce is a bisque with egg yolks, and is usually served over toast, rice, noodles, or various fish (e.g., lobster). The secret to making this sauce is to stir constantly. It can curdle and lump up, and will make a terrible mess if you don't. This is a very rich dish, both in calories and in cost.

You can precook the shrimp by steaming, boiling, or microwaving, but it is worthwhile to save the peelings to make a shrimp butter. (Cover the peels with water, boil for 5 minutes, and then strain out the shells. Reduce the liquid and add to melted butter.)

INGREDIENTS

1 pound peeled, cooked shrimp

3 tablespoons butter or margarine

2 tablespoons chopped Bermuda onion

2 tablespoons chopped fresh chives

2 tablespoons all-purpose flour

3 cups milk

1/2 cup heavy cream

About 2 tablespoons dry sherry or to taste

Paprika

White pepper

1-1/2 tablespoons fresh chopped tarragon or 2 teaspoons dried; or fresh or dried dill, basil, lemon balm, or savory

2 egg yolks

. . . .

Melt 2 tablespoons of the butter in a large heavy pot. Mix the onions and chives with remaining butter and microwave on high for about 2 minutes to soften; set aside. Stir the flour into the butter in the pot and brown it over low heat. While stirring constantly with a wire whisk, slowly add the milk and heat to almost a boil, then lower to a simmer, and keep stirring. Slowly add the cream and shrimp (keep stirring), and simmer for a couple minutes more. Add the onion mix, sherry, paprika, pepper, and herbs. Stir in the egg yolks and cook for another minute or so.

JAMBALAYA

Serves 4

To many people—my wife included—this is the pride of Cajun cooking, with good reason.

I N G R E D I E N T S
. . . .

1 pound shrimp

2 slices bacon, chopped

1/2 cup chopped onion

2 garlic cloves, finely chopped

1 small green bell pepper, chopped

3–4 medium tomatoes, peeled, or equivalent canned

1 cup long-grain rice

Chili powder (gentle!)

Fresh or dried basil, marjoram, or oregano to taste

1/2 cup chopped cooked ham

Worcestershire sauce

Louisiana Red Sauce (page 68) or commercial cocktail sauce

71

SHRIMP

Simmer the shrimp in water to cover until pink, about 1 minute. Remove from broth, clean, and refrigerate. Strain the broth and reduce by half. Fry the bacon in a heavy pot and set aside. Sauté the onion, garlic, and green pepper in the bacon drippings. Add the shrimp broth, tomatoes, rice, and seasonings. Bring to a boil, cover, and simmer until the rice is tender, about 25 minutes. Stir frequently, as it will stick if you are not attentive. Add a little water or white wine if necessary to keep moist. Add the ham, bacon, and shrimp in the last few moments of cooking, just to warm them. Serve with Worcestershire and hot sauce. Okra and cornbread are traditional side dishes.

SHRIMP MARINARA

Serves 3 or 4

I N G R E D I E N T S

1 clove garlic

2 tablespoons olive oil

1 small onion, chopped

2 small to medium tomatoes, peeled and chopped

8-ounce can tomato sauce

1/4 cup dry sherry

3/4 pound medium shrimp (about 20 count), cleaned

1/2 teaspoon sugar

1/4 teaspoon dried herbs (oregano, basil, marjoram, savory)

12 ounces spaghetti, cooked

Grated Parmesan cheese

P R O C E D U R E

Brown the garlic in olive oil in a large, heavy cast-iron skillet, about 5 minutes. Crush the clove to release juice, then discard. Sauté the onion until soft, about 3 minutes, then add the tomatoes, tomato sauce, sherry and about 1/3 of the shrimp, finely chopped. Bring to a boil, then simmer for 15 to 20 minutes, stirring continually to prevent scorching. You may need to add a little water from time to time to prevent overthickening. Add the sugar and herbs, and cook for 2 to 3 minutes; taste and adjust the seasonings. Stir in the remaining shrimp and cook until pink, about 1 minute. Serve over the hot spaghetti with Parmesan cheese.

SHRIMP CURRY

Serves 4 or 5

I include this recipe for those with galvanized intestinal tracts. Personally, I don't like curry, but here it is.

I N G R E D I E N T S

1 pound cleaned medium shrimp
1-inch piece cinnamon stick
1 garlic clove
4 dashes Louisiana Red Sauce (page 73)
Pinch of turmeric

1 slice ginger, chopped (or 1/4 teaspoon ground)
1 small onion, sliced
1/3 cup coconut milk or water
1/2 tablespoon corn oil
2 tablespoons fresh lime juice

P R O C E D U R E

Combine shrimp with the cinnamon, garlic, Louisiana red sauce, turmeric, ginger, and half the onion in a large pan. Add the coconut milk or water and simmer until shrimp is almost pink—about 1 minute. (It is firm and white on the outside but it isn't pink yet.) Set aside. Sauté the remaining onion in the oil until soft, about 3 minutes, then add to the shrimp and stir in lime juice. Simmer for 5 minutes or so, then serve over rice.

Note: In Indian restaurants curries are usually served with a regional flat bread called a chapatti, which resemble tortillas in consistency but is made from wheat; they are available in most Eastern or Indian markets.

73

SHRIMP PIZZA SNACK

This is less a recipe than a tasty suggestion for a quick snack for parties. Proportions are what you wish. My preference is about 3 small shrimp, 1 piece of cooked bacon, 1/2 tablespoon of tomato sauce, and 1 thin slice of cheese (plus whatever additional tidbits happen by) for each muffin half.

INGREDIENTS

English muffins (or pita loaves)
Pizza sauce
Thin-sliced cheese
Minced dried oregano
Cooked bacon pieces
Cleaned and cooked small shrimp (canned or frozen are quite
good, but warm the frozen or drain the canned)
Olive oil
Sliced fresh mushrooms
Sliced sweet onion
Sliced stuffed green olives

PROCEDURE

Preheat the oven to 400° F. for large quantities but a toaster oven will make 6 or 8 muffin halves (usually enough to stave off hunger pangs for 2 while more cook). Split the muffins, place on a baking sheet, spread with pizza sauce, and add slices of cheese. You may wish to add mushroom and/or onion slices at this point, too. Sprinkle with bacon bits and top with the shrimp. Sprinkle lightly with olive oil. Other optional ingredients except the olive slices can also be added at this point. Bake or broil until the cheese melts, remove from heat, and top with the olive slices.

FRIED SHRIMP

Serves 2 or 3

I would very much like to register a complaint about the way most fish is pre-pared in Florida—that is, fried. Almost everywhere you go the fish is over-cooked in a heavy batter that virtually destroys the taste. Shrimp, which are also treated in this manner, especially bring tears to my eyes. But deep-fried shrimp can be savory, as the following recipe shows.

INGREDIENTS

Vegetable oil for deep-frying

30 medium shrimp

1 cup flour (half all-purpose and half rice flour, if possible)

1 teaspoon baking powder

2 teaspoons crumbled dried tarragon or dill, marjoram, or savory

1 or 2 large eggs (crispier crust with 2)

PROCEDURE

Heat the oil to 400° F. Peel and clean the shrimp, saving the shells. Boil shells in water to cover, then strain out the shells, and reserve the liquid. Mix the flours, baking powder, tarragon, and eggs in a large bowl. Add enough of the shrimp liquid to make a batter that will stick to the shrimp when you dip them. A thin batter gives a light coat to the finished food, while a thicker one gives a puffier crust. You control the crust thickness by the amount of liquid you add. Dip the shrimp in the batter and drop into the hot oil. When the crust browns, in about 1 minute, take the shrimp out and drain on brown bags or paper towels. Serve with cocktail sauce, tartar sauce, or even ketchup.

CRABS

AND

LOBSTERS

CRABS

C rab and lobster are two of the most popular seafoods. You can buy just the meat of these delicious crustaceans, but it is more likely that you will encounter the entire animals. The vast majority of crabs and lobsters are prepared in the simplest way imaginable—dropped in boiling water until they turn red, then their meat is picked from the shell and dipped in melted butter by the diner. Fancier preparations usually call for first boiling them, the notable exception being for Maryland soft-shell crab.

MARYLAND
SOFT SHELL CRAB

Vegetable oil for deep-frying
2 soft-shell crabs per person
Batter of choice (pages 22–23)

Heat the oil to 375° F. Wash the crabs under cold running water. Coat the crabs with the batter (thicker batter gives a fluffier coat), then drop one at a time into the hot oil. When the crabs are browned, in about 2 minutes, they are ready to eat. Drain on paper towels or brown paper (help reduce land fill pollution by using supermarket brown bags). The better restaurants serve soft shells on toast points. Simply eat them whole; don't bother with what is what.

77

CRABS
AND
LOBSTERS

CRAB SALAD

Make 16 to 20 hors d'oeuvres

Crab is a very delicate meat, so any heavy herbs are out. You may want to add a touch of tarragon or dill, or even a teaspoon of very mild onion (scallion, shallots), but be careful not to overdo.

Either purchase lump crab meat or boil crabs and extract their meat from the shells. It takes me about 40 minutes to thoroughly pick a crab—about 2 hours to clean 3 crabs to get 1 cup of meat. You might consider buying crab meat.

INGREDIENTS

1 cup crab meat
1/2 cup chopped celery
1/2 cup chopped hard apple

3 tablespoons mayonnaise
4–5 slices toast

PROCEDURE

Combine the first 4 ingredients. Cut toast into points by slicing diagonally corner to corner each way. Spread with the crab mix.

CRABS IN SPAGHETTI SAUCE

Rock crabs, green crabs, and other small crabs that are usually ignored can give a delicious touch to an otherwise bland spaghetti sauce.

INGREDIENTS

Crabs (any quantity and most types available)
1 32-ounce jar commercial meatless spaghetti sauce
1 pound pasta, cooked

Steam the crabs and pick the meat from the main shell. If the legs and claws look large enough to bother eating at the table, set them aside; otherwise extract what meat you can and discard the shells. Add the crab meat to the spaghetti sauce and simmer for 1-1/2 to 2 hours. Heat the reserved crab legs in the sauce for the last 5 to 10 minutes, just to warm them. Serve over hot pasta.

LOBSTER

Recipes for shrimp are also excellent for lobster. Just boil a lobster, extract the meat, and substitute for shrimp in a recipe. Lobster has a unique and highly prized flavor, which the following recipes show off expecially well. In ascending order of calories:

BOILED LOBSTER

B oiling is the first step in almost all lobster preparations. It is also an excellent way to enjoy lobster.

I · · N · · · G · · · R · · · E · · · · D · · · · I · · · E · · · N · · · T · · · S

1–2 lobsters per person (1-1/4 pound weight each)
Butter, melted

P · · R · · · O · · · C · · · · E · ' · D · · · · U · · · R · · · · E

Fill a large pot with water and bring to a boil. Drop a live lobster into the water. When the lobster turns red, in about 2 minutes, it is cooked. Serve lobsters with melted butter and large napkins (messy). Baked potato and corn on the cob are traditional accompaniments.

BAKED STUFFED LOBSTER

Serves 4

This, to me, is No. 1. The tomalley (soft green stuff) found in the body cavity of female lobsters makes a good stuffing great.

INGREDIENTS

4 lobsters

8 ounces Ritz crackers, crushed

2 celery stalks, finely chopped

3/4 cup picked crab, shrimp,
   or lobster meat

1/2 cup (1 stick) butter

1/2 teaspoon dried dill

4 large lettuce leaves

1-1/2 teaspoons lemon juice

PROCEDURE

Boil the lobsters until done, about 2 minutes. Place on a large tray or baking sheet with lip to catch the juice, and cool. Mix crackers, celery, and seafood in a mixing bowl. Split the lobsters from head to tail. Scoop out the tomalley (and coral, if there is any), and add the tomalley to the stuffing mix. The stuffing may be a bit dry; if so, add a little melted butter. Mix in the dill and fill the body halves with the stuffing, mounding slightly. Cover the stuffed lobsters with lettuce leaves. Put under the broiler for about 4 minutes. Combine the remaining butter and the lemon juice over low heat to make lemon butter. Take the lobsters from the oven and remove the lettuce leaves. Return to the broiler only long enough to brown the top of the stuffing—another minute or two. Serve with individual dishes of hot lemon butter.

LOBSTER THERMIDOR

Serves 4

This is a bit more complicated than simple boiled lobster, and rather rich, although not as heavy as a Newburg.

4 1-1/4 pound lobsters

4 tablespoons (1/2 stick) butter

2 tablespoons all-purpose flour

1/2 cup cream

Fresh herbs, such as dill or tarragon (optional)

1 tablespoon finely chopped mild onion (optional)

8 ounces Ritz crackers, crushed

Sprinkling of cognac

P R O C E D U R E

Boil the lobsters and save the water. Extract the meat and finely chop. Place the shells back in the cooking water, and boil the water down to make about 2 cups of stock. Strain and set shells in a broil pan for later.

Make a roux with 2 tablespoons butter and the flour, cooking for a couple of minutes to remove the raw flour taste. Place the roux in a double boiler over boiling water and slowly blend in lobster meat, cream, and stock. If desired, add a teaspoon or so of fresh herbs. Simmer the sauce, stirring frequently, for about 10 minutes to thicken somewhat. Meanwhile, soften the onion in the remaining butter. Add onions and crackers to sauce and stir. Stuff the lobster shells with this mix. Sprinkle a few drops of cognac on each lobster, and broil just enough to brown the tops, about 1 minute.

LOBSTER NEWBURG

Serves 4

N ot recommended for the cholesterol or calorie conscious. Incidentally, shrimp or crab are great substitutes for the lobster.

I N G R E D I E N T S

4 tablespons (1/2 stick) butter

2 cups diced lobster meat

1/4 cup dry sherry

3 large egg yolks

1 cup heavy cream

1 teaspoon chopped fresh tarragon or dill (optional)

P R O C E D U R E

Melt the butter in a heavy pan and add the lobster meat. Cook gently for 3 to 4 minutes, or until the lobster flavor blends with the butter. Add the sherry and continue cooking for a couple minutes longer. Beat the egg yolks and cream together in a double boiler. (Don't take a chance; cook over boiling water and the temperature will stay low enough to avoid scorching). Add the lobster to the cream and mix. Add fresh herbs to season the sauce, if desired, then stir over low heat until it thickens. Serve over plain boiled rice.

FISH
COOKERY

TEN
. . . .

SNAILS

. . . .
Have you ever had Manhattan-style chowder in Manhattan? If so, and your experience was like mine, you've already eaten at least one kind of snail (whelk), and probably found it tough. Don't blame the snail: the fault was all the cook's. Sea snails (such as whelks, conchs, moon snails, and periwinkles) and land snails (such as the famous escargot) can be very tasty and tender. The trick is preparation. Wash the snails thoroughly under running water, then parboil in a baking soda and water (1/2 cup of soda to a gallon of water) solution until the snails are easily pulled from their shells. Drain them and let cool until you can handle them comfortably, but *don't rinse*. The operculum (the trap door the snail

uses to close its shell) and shell can be discarded, unless you wish to preserve specimens as the museums do. (To make your own museum specimen, rinse the shell and operculum in fresh water; dry and stuff the shell with cotton batting. Glue the operculum to the cotton in its original position.) Parboil the snail meat for 5 minutes in fresh water. Drain, cool, and chop up if necessary. The meat can now be used in any clam recipe.

Note: If you plan to cook snails in the South Pacific, check with a native before you try unfamiliar ones. Some snails in those seas are deadly.

SNAIL SALAD

One conch serves 4

Caribbean islanders prepare conch (a very large and tough snail) by placing it in lime juice for 10 days to 2 weeks. This has the same effect as boiling, but the meat is much more tender. Native women further tenderize these large snails by putting them on a log and beating them with a stick. Smaller snails are simply boiled and their digestive tracts removed.

INGREDIENTS

Vinaigrette dressing made with olive oil and lime juice

Equal quantities of: chopped celery, carrots, onions, and snail meat

1/4 quantity chopped pimiento (optional)

Sliced green bell pepper (optional)

Chopped olives (optional)

Chopped fresh herbs (tarragon, dill, parsley)

PROCEDURE

To a basic vinaigrette add the remaining ingredients except the herbs, and marinate for 2 days in the refrigerator. Drain and add herbs just before serving. (Do not put the fresh herbs in the refrigerator mix or they will become bitter.) Serve with German pumpernickel bread and bits of Swiss cheese or crisp crackers.

CONCH FRITTERS

Serves 6

Since conchs are large, *tough* creatures, parting them from their homes is not easy. To make fritters, boil them for 20 to 30 minutes; at this point any resemblance to shoe leather is normal. Cut out and discard the digestive tract (the dark portion). Then put the meat through a meat grinder *twice*. The meat is now ready to make delicious fritters.

I N G R E D I E N T S

Vegetable oil, for deep-frying
2 cups well-ground snail meat
Batter of choice (pages 22–23), made with double measure of flour or commercial mix.

P R O C E D U R E

Preheat oil to at least 400° F. Mix ingredients in a 2-quart mixing bowl, adding sufficient liquid to make a thick batter. Drop in rounded teaspoonfuls into hot oil and deep-fry for 2 minutes or until crisp and lightly browned. Serve with either tartar sauce or shrimp cocktail sauce.

CONCHBURGERS

Serves 4 to 6

I N G R E D I E N T S

1/2 cup minced onion
1 cup diced celery
2 tablespoons (1/4 stick) margarine
2 cups well-ground snail meat

1/4 cup diced green bell pepper (optional)

1-1/2 cups unseasoned bread crumbs

2 large eggs

Tarragon, basil, oregano, parsley, or other seasoning to taste

P R O C E D U R E

Soften the onion and celery with a bit of margarine in the microwave for 2 minutes. Mix onion and celery with snail meat, pepper, and bread crumbs in a medium bowl. Beat the eggs separately, then mix with ingredients in bowl and add seasoning. Form into patties and pan-fry, oven broil, or grill until done, about 3 minutes.

Note: If grilling, sprinkle with a little lime juice for a different treat.

SNAIL-STUFFED MUSHROOMS

Serves 6

I N G R E D I E N T S

1-1/2 tablespoons butter	Chopped fresh herbs (tarragon, basil)
4 tablespoons all-purpose flour	9 large mushroom caps
1-1/2 cups chicken stock	Dry sherry (just a few drops)
2 cups well-ground snail meat	Toast, parsley sprigs, or crisp bacon for garnish

P R O C E D U R E

Preheat the broiler. Make a roux by melting the butter in a heavy saucepan and and blending in flour. Cook for a bit, about 3 minutes, then slowly blend in the stock. Stir over a slow heat to make a sauce, then stir in the snail meat and herbs. Thicken the sauce by stirring constantly over low heat with a wire whisk. Coat the mushroom caps with butter and place open side up on a greased baking sheet. Fill the caps with the snail mixture, then broil for about 5 minutes. Sprinkle on a few drops of sherry, and serve the the mushroom caps on toast slices garnished with parsley, and/or bacon.

Note: Any extra stuffing can be served as is or as an accompaniment.

COLD
SEAS
FINFISH

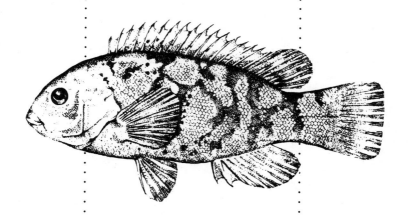

BLACKFISH

(TAUTOG)

There are relatively few species found in cold waters, but there are many individuals of each species. Most are either white, mild-flavored fish or darker, highly flavored fish. The recipes for cod, flounder, blackfish, and hake are pretty much interchangeable except when the size of the fillets makes one particular cooking style more appropriate. The highly flavored fish are usually also interchangeable with each other, except in special cases.

Blackfish resemble blue perch but are larger and heavier. They live around rock piles in strictly coastal waters, although sometimes they are found over mussel beds as far as three or four miles from shore—but not farther. They prefer steep rocky shores, ledges, wrecks, piers, breakwaters, and boulders. Since the areas where they live are not amenable to net fishing, they are largely ignored by commercial interests. The name blackfish is also commonly used for the black sea bass, which generally ranges farther offshore than the tautog. They are often available in good fish markets in the spring and fall. The flavor of these fish is distinctive and lends itself exceptionally well to such dishes as Blackfish chowder (page 92), Blackfish à l'Orange (page 91), and other recipes with relatively heavy spices and herbs. Whole fish possess lateral line bones that must be removed in filleting.

BLACKFISH FINGERS

A quick, simple, and tasty way to prepare blackfish.

I N G R E D I E N T S

1 2-pound blackfish
1 cup seasoned bread crumbs
3 tablespoons clarified butter

P R O C E D U R E

Fillet and skin the fish. Watch out for lateral line bones, as they run quite far back. Run your finger along the lateral line to feel where the bones are, and remove them by cutting down close on either side of the lateral line and pulling the bony strip out. Cut the fillets into finger-size strips. Roll in bread crumbs and sauté in clarified butter until done, about 5 minutes. Fish is done when it loses translucence and solidifies. Serve plain, with Tartar sauce (recipe follows), or Louisiana Red Sauce (page 68).

Tartar Sauce

INGREDIENTS

Green pickle relish

Mayonnaise

Seasonings as desired (cardamom, chili powder, or other)

PROCEDURE

Mix 3 parts relish to 1 part mayonnaise, then add desired seasoning.

Blackfish à l'Orange

Serves 4

Tuna or bluefish also go well in this recipe.

2 cups orange juice

2 tablespoons soy sauce

2 teaspoons minced garlic

1-1/2 teaspoons ground cumin
or chili powder

2 pounds blackfish fillets

Make a marinade of the first 4 ingredients. Marinate the fillets in the regfrigerator for from 2 to 12 hours. Drain, then broil or sauté. Serve with boiled small white potatoes and buttered asparagus.

BLACKFISH CHOWDER

Serves 4

B ecause the flavor of this fish is unique, it deserves special mention for a fish chowder. Starting with a basic chowder recipe, add a little chili powder and basil. Do not use milk, as it gives an off flavor. Tomatoes and peppers should be sparingly used if at all. Instead, the onion family—garlic, leeks, shallots, chives, onions—is excellent, but use with discretion as the flavor of the fish is both subtle and somewhat delicate. Serve steaming dishes of Blackfish chowder with buttered sea crackers and watch the meal disappear.

VEGI-STUFFED BLACKFISH

Serves 4

1/2 small onion, finely chopped

1 tablespoon minced green bell pepper

2 tablespoons (1/4 stick) margarine

1-1/2 cups cracker crumbs

3/4 cup bread crumbs

1/2 cup cooked lima beans

1/2 cup chopped steamed squash (any kind)

1-1/2–2 pounds blackfish fillets

Parsley flakes

Paprika

Lemon juice

P R O C E D U R E

Preheat the oven to 350° F. Coat a large glass baking dish with non-stick vegetable spray. Sauté onion and green pepper in the margarine until soft, about 3 minutes. Mix crumbs and blend in a bowl with onion, pepper, lima beans, and squash. Stuffing should be moderately dry; add more crumbs if too wet, a little water if too dry. Place the fillets in the baking dish and pack the stuffing over the top. Sprinkle with parsley flakes and paprika, then bake until the fish appears done when inspected from below, about 3 to 5 minutes. Drizzle a few drops of lemon juice over each fish before serving.

SPINACH AND FETA-STUFFED BLACKFISH

Serves 3 to 4

I N G R E D I E N T S

2 pounds blackfish fillets

2 cups chopped fresh spinach

1/4 pound ripe pitted black olives, diced

1/4 pound feta cheese

1/4 pound crackers, crushed

2 tablespoons (1/4 stick) margarine or butter

1/2 teaspoon lime juice

93

BLACKFISH
(TAUTOG)

· ·

Preheat the oven to 350° F. Cut the fillets horizontally to 1/8 inch thickness. Put half the fillets a single layer in a medium glass baking dish. Mix the spinach, olives, cheese, and cracker crumbs in a bowl to make stuffing. Put a layer of stuffing over the fillets, then add another layer of blackfish and another layer of stuffing. Bake for about 10 minutes. Melt the butter with the lime juice. Take the fish from the oven and sprinkle the lime butter over the top, then return fish to the oven for another 5 minutes. The top should be barely browned and the fish will appear white through the glass.

BLACK SEA BASS

B lack sea bass (also called sea bass or blackfish), like its cousins the striper bass and white perch, is a lean, mild-flavored white fish. It is relatively small, usually only massing two or three pounds, so the fillets are roughly the size of flounder fillets. Any of the flounder recipes are fine for this fish, but we found the following casserole especially good for this fish.

BLACK SEA BASS CASSEROLE

Serves 4

· ·

1 pound black sea bass fillets

Fresh tarragon leaves

Dry sherry

1/4–1/2 pound fresh mushrooms, thinly sliced

1 pound green beans, cooked (broccoli is a superb alternative)

1 10-ounce can condensed cream of mushroom soup

1 large fresh tomato, thickly sliced

1/4 pound grating cheese such as Parmesan

4 slices firm thin white bread

Butter

Paprika

P R O C E D U R E

Preheat the oven to 350° F. Cover the bottom of a medium oiled glass baking dish with fillets. Sprinkle tarragon and sherry lightly over the fish, then layer the mushrooms. Add the beans, and cover with the condensed soup. Next add tomato slices, and grate the cheese over the top. Butter the toast and cut into 1/8-inch cubes. Scatter the cubes over the dish, then lightly sprinkle with paprika. Bake for 20 to 25 minutes, or until the fish turns white. (Look up from the bottom of the dish.)

SCUP

The scup or northern porgy, a common visitor to New England waters in the summer, is a highly sought fish. It is more flavorful than cod, usually marketed whole, since cleaning them properly is a job most people prefer to avoid. The fish are relatively small (eight to fourteen inches long) and have lateral line bones that must be removed to make skinless fillets. The pieces of boneless fish are, consequently, quite small, so most people just grill the cleaned whole fish.

Porgy lacks the firmness of cold-water fish such as cod; the flesh is closer to that of crab meat. For this reason, I prefer to slice the meat into little fingers which can then be dipped in batter and deep-fried. Some of my friends prefer to dip the fillets in beaten egg, roll them in seasoned flour, and then deep-fry them. The latter process shows more of the fish's flavor, but the former gives a much more desirable texture. The fillets are also good in chowders or soups.

Southern cousins of this popular little fish run much larger and in a variety of colors, but they are the same fish for all practical purposes. The flavor of the southern cousins is a bit stronger, so you may wish to use a marinade to mellow it.

Because the fillets are small, such methods as baking and broiling are not recommended. Poaching or batter deep-frying are much easier to control. A particularly interesting preparation is Porgies David (below), although the recipe for White Perch Dijon (page 132) also works well with this fish.

PORGIES DAVID

Serves 4 to 6

3 tablespoons lemon juice

1/2 cup mayonnaise

Sprinkling of black pepper

Pinch of dried dill

Dash of herbal seasoning mix (Mrs. Dash is very good)

2 pounds porgy fillets, deboned

1 cup Ritz crackers

Preheat the oven to 500° F. Make a marinade of the lemon juice, mayonnaise, black pepper, dill, and herbal seasoning mix. You can also add tarragon but not garlic, as it grows stronger with cooking and will destroy the flavor balances.

Marinate the fillets for 10 to 20 minutes. Crush the crackers very finely by rolling them between sheets of wax paper with a rolling pin or pass them through a food processor. Coat a large glass baking pan with a non-stick vegetable spray. Pat the fillets with paper towels, roll in cracker crumbs, and arrange in pan in a single layer. Bake for 10 to 15 minutes, or until fish flakes or loses its translucency and turns white. Visual montoring works quite well with a glass baking pan. If the top also has a brownish crust, the fish is perfect. Do not overcook; overdone fish is best donated to your friendly neighborhood cobbler.

TWELVE

BLUEFISH

The bluefish of New England and the bluefish of the South are so different as to be virtually different species. In northern waters the principal diet for these fish is members of the herring family, which are rather oily and strong in flavor. This strong flavor is imparted to the flesh of the bluefish. Consequently, the northern bluefish demands extreme care on the part of the fisherman preparatory to cooking. I use a large barrel of cold seawater in which to bleed the fish immediately after catching. This eliminates most of the strong taste. Another good move is to ice the fish as soon as it has been bled. Further, when I prepare the fillets for cooking, I cut out the very dark blood-line meat.

BROILED STUFFED BLUEFISH

INGREDIENTS

1/2 pound bluefish fillet per person
Lemon juice
Soy sauce
Butter

Bluefish Stuffing (recipe follows)
Grated cheese
Fresh parsley, for garnish

PROCEDURE

Preheat the broiler. Lay the fillets on a large baking platter with a gravy moat. Baste with lemon juice and/or soy sauce, and dot with butter. Mix enough dressing to cover the bluefish by about 1/2 inch. Cover loosely with aluminum foil and place under the broiler for about 15 minutes. Remove the platter, take off the stuffing, and return fish to the broiler to brown, about 2 minutes. Remove from heat, replace the stuffing, sprinkle with grated cheese, and return briefly to the broiler to brown. Melt cheese, about 1 minute. Garnish with parsley.

BLUEFISH STUFFING

Easily serves 4

Bluefish goes exceedingly well with whipped salad dressing (or mayonnaise) as well as lemon, soy sauce, green peppers, garlic, onions, tomato, and/or cheese. Try these seasonings alone or in combinations.

INGREDIENTS

4 slices high-quality white bread
2 garlic cloves or 1 large onion, finely minced
1/2 pound fresh mushrooms, sliced

1 celery stalk, finely chopped

3 fresh basil or lemon verbena leaves

1 cup steamed mussel meat; crab meat or lobster; or chopped steamed scallops

1/2 cup (1 stick) butter or margarine

1 large egg

1/4 teaspoon chili powder

P R O C E D U R E

Chop the bread into tiny cubes and put in a large bowl. Add the garlic or onion, sliced mushrooms (canned are marginally acceptable), celery, herbs, and seafood. Melt the butter and add, together with egg and chili powder.

QUICK BLUEFISH STUFFING

Serves 4

With considerable embarrassment and reluctance I include a lazy version. In Greece they soak 1/2 cup raisins in warm water until they swell to triple size, drain off the liquid, and add the raisins to the stuffing. Unfortunately, the stuffing is no longer quite so quick.

I N G R E D I E N T S

2 small packages prepared bread crumbs

1-1/2 pounds cooked and cleaned small shrimp, chopped

1/2 cup (1 stick) butter, melted

1 large egg

P R O C E D U R E

Put the crumbs in a large bowl, add the shrimp and butter, and stir in egg.

99

BLUEFISH CHEEKS WITH BUTTER AND ONIONS

Serves 2 to 4

Commercial bluefish cleaners cut the two large fillets from the body and throw the rest away. The cheeks of the fish, however, are highly prized by knowledgeable fisherman; in fact, one friend eats only the cheeks and gives the rest away. These half-dollar size chunks of meat reach only a 1/2-inch thickness at best, so it takes a number of fish to make a meal.

INGREDIENTS

1 medium onion
Butter or margarine

12–14 bluefish cheeks

PROCEDURE

Slice the onion, coat a large skillet with non-stick vegetable spray, then add the butter, and sauté the onions and fish together for 3 minutes or until the cheeks turn white. Serve with garlic bread and sautéed asparagus tips.

ROSIE'S BLUEFISH ITALIANO

Serves 6

Here is a zingy version of Italian bluefish.

INGREDIENTS

2 garlic cloves
1 cup olive or corn oil
1 lemon, halved and seeded

1 bunch parsley, preferably Italian flat
3/4 cup vermouth or other white wine
3–4 pounds bluefish fillets

Sauté the garlic in the oil just until lightly brown, about 2 minutes. Flatten the cloves and cook in the oil for a few seconds longer, then remove and discard. Pour the oil into a bowl. Chop the lemon finely. Add the lemon pulp, peel, and juice to the oil. Chop the parsley and add to the oil. Stir in the vermouth.

Marinate the fish overnight or at least several hours in the refrigerator. Preheat the oven to 350° F. Place fish in baking dish and bake for 30 to 45 minutes, or until it flakes when pricked with a fork.

BEER-BATTERED
BLUEFISH CHEEKS

Make Beer Batter(page 22). Dip the cheeks in batter and deep-fry at 450 F. for half a minute. Serve with tartar sauce.

BLUEFISH CUBION

Serves 4+

This is a Carribbean taste treat worth trying.

2 bunches scallions, or equivalent onions, leeks, or shallots

2 tablespoons olive oil

1/2 pound fresh mushrooms, chopped

3 tablespoons tomato paste

3 pounds bluefish fillets, cut in 3/4-inch cubes

2 tablespoons all-purpose flour

1 tablespoon lard

About 1-1/2 cups water

P   R   O   C   E   D   U   R   E

Chop the scallions fine. Put olive oil in a large iron skillet over a moderate heat. Add the scallions and sauté until they are almost done, about 5 minutes. Add the mushrooms and continue cooking for a minute or two, then blend in the tomato paste. Add the bluefish and set the pan off the heat for the moment. The fish will continue to cook in the hot sauce.

To prepare an authentic New Orleans roux, fry the flour and lard until the mixture is browned, about 15 minutes. Don't undercook, as this step is critical to removing the raw taste of the flour. Remove from the heat and use a wire whisk to blend in the water. (Block Island dwellers prefer milk, while I like a mild white wine. If you happen to have some leftover cooking liquid from shrimp, crab, or lobster, use that.) Add the roux to the fish mix and slowly blend in, using more water over a low heat to make a fairly thick sauce. Stir constantly until smooth. Serve over rice or toast points for a treat to remember.

BLUEFISH SALAD

A "tuna" salad that bypasses ordinary canned tuna.

I   N   G   R   E   D   I   E   N   T   S

4–6 ounces cooked bluefish meat per serving

Ingredients for your favorite tuna salad (celery, onion, and mayonnaise or salad dressing)

P   R   O   C   E   D   U   R   E

If you have leftover broiled stuffed fish and dressing, throw it in a bowl with stuffing, chopped onion, celery, and salad dressing and mix.

When I have raw frozen or fresh fish, I put it in a steamer or microwave it until it falls apart, discard the liquid, and carefully (watch out for bones; even I sometimes slip and leave one for my wife . . . at least that's what she claims) flake the meat into a bowl. I then add the other ingredients and mix.

Lemon verbena or lemon juice is a tasty addition, but use discreetly. You may also wish to trim the dark strip from the fillet. Its flavor is much stronger than the rest.

BLUEFISH CHEEKS WITH MUSHROOMS AND SHERRY

Serves 1

This is a tasty snack for one. Just increase the ingredients for more people or hunger.

INGREDIENTS

1 tablespoon butter
2 bluefish cheeks
4 small fresh mushrooms, sliced
1 teaspoon dry sherry

PROCEDURE

Melt the butter in a heavy pan. Cut the cheeks into slices about as wide as thick, then put in the butter and sauté, about 3 minutes. Turn heat to low, turn the cheeks over, and add the mushrooms. Saute another 3 minutes, then add the sherry. Simmer for a couple of minutes, then serve with cheddar cheese slices or wheat thin crackers.

BAKED BLUEFISH WITH
SOUR CREAM AND MUSSSELS

Serves 4

INGREDIENTS

2 pounds bluefish fillets

1-1/2 pints sour cream

1 pound mussels

1/4 pound Ritz crackers, crushed

2 tablespoons butter or margarine

1/2 tablespoon lemon juice

1 tablespoon minced tarragon leaves

Sprinkling of dry sherry

1 medium onion, chopped

1/2 cup chopped mushrooms

PROCEDURE

Marinate the fillets in sour cream for 1-1/2 to 2 hours. Steam the mussels, pull them from their shells, and discard their byssal threads. Chop the meats and mix with crackers. Adjust texture with lemon butter and add tarragon leaves and a little dry sherry. Microwave chopped onion and mushrooms for 2 minutes on high. Add to mussel mixture. Preheat the oven to 350° F. Pat the fish dry and lay in a large glass baking dish. Cover with 1/4-inch layer of sour cream, then with the mussel stuffing. Bake until the fish flakes on the fork test.

BLUEFISH SASHIMI

Traditional Japanese cuisine calls for raw tuna, but here is a tasty substitute made with bluefish.

1 part soy sauce

1 part chicken broth

1 part oriental hot mustard

Partly frozen bluefish fillets

Mix soy sauce, broth, and mustard to make sushi sauce. Thinly slice the fillets. To serve, dip slices in sauce and serve with melba rounds or some other cracker or bread.

Note: As always, avoid fish from polluted waters.

CRACKER BLUEFISH

A 3-pound bluefish fillet should comfortably serve 4

Cook bluefish Cracker Style (page 25), and you'll have one of the great outdoor dishes. It is not absolutely necessary to use the grapefruit juice; some people prefer to smother the fish with assorted vegetables and cook in aluminum foil. Typical vegetable choices are onions, garlic, tomatoes, and mushrooms. Other popular additions are mussels, oysters, and fresh herbs such as tarragon and dill. All are well worth trying.

JERK BLUEFISH

A fillet from a 12-pound fish easily feeds 4.

Jerk spices are well suited to bluefish. Simply sprinkle fillets with jerk spices (page 26), dot with butter, and broil. Corn on the cob and baked potato or french fries are excellent accompaniments.

Smoked Bluefish Salad

Serves 2

3/4 cup mayonnaise

1/4 cup sour cream

1-1/2 cups flaked smoked bluefish

2 celery stalks, chopped

1 small onion, chopped

1 bunch scallions, chopped

Prepared horseradish

Tabasco sauce

Mix mayonnaise and sour cream. Mix the bluefish with the celery, onion, and scallions. Moisten with the sour cream-mayonnaise mixture and adjust seasoning by adding horseradish and Tabasco to taste.

THIRTEEN

COD

For cooking purposes, cod, pollock, and haddock are essentially the same fish. Scrod is the term to describe the young fish of all three species. The unique flavor of haddock, which makes it so sought after, disperses quickly, which is probably why the fish is marketed with its skin on so that you can see that it is really haddock. If the fish is very fresh, broil it with only margarine or butter. The flavor of the fish is so delicate that any additions overwhelm it.

Pollock, which is marketed as Boston bluefish, doesn't keep as well frozen as either cod or haddock, and is usually rather dark in color in the supermarket. (The dark color indicates a beginning stage of rot.) Likewise, beading of moisture on the surface or any objectional odor also indicates that the fish would be better given to your neighbor's cats.

These recipes apply to all of these fish, but are also highly adaptable to any other lean, mild-flavored fish, such as cusk. Scrod is, of course, much milder in flavor and more tender than adult fish.

SPUDDED COD

Serves 4

We first discovered this dish with fillets that had been frozen for eight months. The fish tasted fresh.

I N G R E D I E N T S

2 pounds fresh or frozen cod fillets

1 cup mashed potato flakes

1 teaspoon finely chopped fresh tarragon, dill, or basil

1 large egg beaten with 1 tablespoon powdered milk and 2 tablespoons water

4 tablespoons (1/2 stick) margarine, melted

Approximately 2 teaspoons lemon juice

P R O C E D U R E

Thaw the fillets if frozen. Preheat the oven to 500° F. Place the potato flakes and herbs in a bowl and mix. Dip the fish in the egg mix and then roll it in the potato mix. Arrange the fillets in a shallow baking dish. Mix the melted butter and lemon juice, and pour over the fish. Bake for 10 minutes, remove from oven, and put under the broiler to brown top side. Turn the fish and brown on the other side, another minute. The fish should now flake on fork-testing.

BROILED FRESH COD

Serves 4

The less done to a fresh-caught fish, the better. Cod that has been caught the same day is magnificent broiled with only lemon-garlic butter.

4 tablespoons (1/2 stick) butter

2 teaspoons lemon juice

1 garlic clove

2 pounds fresh cod fillets

Melt the butter in a frying pan. Add the lemon juice, then heat the garlic for 2 minutes and remove. Just a single clove of garlic should be more than enough.

Place the fish in a single layer in a broil pan. Cover lightly with the lemon-garlic butter, and broil until fish flakes when pricked with a fork, about 2 minutes.

Note: Tarragon butter and dill butter are equally delicious. To make either, use 1 teaspoon herbs to 3 tablespoons melted butter.

CODFISH QUICHE

Serves 6

Actually, scallops, crab, or lobster make a better quiche, but some of us live within a budget. Besides, alliteration is fun. Any fish or shellfish would adapt nicely with only minor seasoning adjustments.

Basic Pastry (page 21)

1 large egg white, lightly beaten

1/4 pound bacon slices

2 cups milk or cream

3 large eggs

1 teaspoon chopped chives

1 pound cooked and flaked codfish fillets

3/4 cup vegetables (optional; see note)

1/2 cup diced Swiss cheese

Preheat the oven to 350° F. Line a quiche pan with the pastry and bake for 10 to 15 minutes, or until the crust is done. Let cool, then brush with egg white.

Turn up the oven to 375°F. Cook the bacon until crisp; drain and dry on paper towels or brown paper. Scald the milk or cream and let cool somewhat. Beat in the eggs and chives; crumble in the bacon, then add the cod, vegetables, and cheese. Mix, then pour into the pastry shell. Bake for 35 to 40 minutes, or until the top is browned.

Note: You may wish to add broccoli or spinach for a more complete dish. Proportions of vegetables are a matter of preference but should not be so generous as to destroy the basic quiche consistency.

WINE-POACHED SCROD

Serves 4

F resh scrod, regardless of how prepared, is delicious. An exceptionally easy and tasty method is to poach it in wine with garlic and parsley. The fish is tender, moist, flaky, and delicious.

I N G R E D I E N T S

2 pounds scrod fillets

1 bottle light dry white wine, such as Reisling

Garlic powder

4 sprigs fresh parsley, for garnish

P R O C E D U R E

Place fillets in a moderately deep sauté pan. Cover to about three-quarters thickness with wine, and sprinkle with garlic powder. Place over moderate heat and bring to a boil. Turn off the heat and cover pan. The fish continues to cook in the hot pan. Garnish with parsley. Green peas and pearl onions are especially nice accompaniments.

SCROD SUPREME

Serves 4

The creative accident is an essential for both jazz musicians and innovative cooks. The trick is to remember what you did so that you can repeat the accidents. This recipe came about because there were little bits of haddock and scallops in the refrigerator, but not enough of either to do very much.

INGREDIENTS

1-1/2 cups cooked haddock fillet
3/4 cup diced bay scallops
3/4 cup seasoned fine bread crumbs
3 tablespoons butter or margarine
1-1/2 pounds scrod fillets

PROCEDURE

Preheat the oven to 375° F. Mix the haddock, scallops, and bread crumbs in a mixing bowl. Melt the butter and add to the mixture. Coat the bottom of a glass baking dish with vegetable spray and add a single layer of scrod. Pack the stuffing over the fillets to a depth of about 1/2 inch. Bake about 10 minutes, or until the fish looks done from underneath. Serve with slices of fresh tomato and green beans.

SCROD PIE

Serves 6

Leftover broiled scrod is toothsome, but when I catch scrod we eat a lot of broiled scrod and cook even more—consequently, we invented the following dish for a succulent change of pace. The other codlike fishes go well in this recipe, too.

. . . .

Basic Pastry (page 21)

1 large egg white, lightly beaten

Approximately 1 pound cooked scrod fillets

1/3 pound cleaned and cooked shrimp

1/3 pound scallops

1 10-ounce can condensed cream of mushroom soup

Paprika

Fresh parsley, for garnish

P R O C E D U R E
. . . .

Preheat the oven to 350° F. Make 6 individual pastry shells, 3-1/2 inches in diameter. Bake the shells for 10 to 15 minutes, or until crisp. Let cool, then brush with egg white.

Flake the fish into a 3-quart mixing bowl. Chop the shrimp and scallops finely, add them to the fish. Stir in the soup, then fill the pastry shells with filling. Sprinkle with paprika and bake for 30 minutes, or until bubbly and lightly browned. Remove from the oven and garnish pies with parsley. You only need a plain vegetable to accompany this.

Lo-Cholesterol Baked Fish

Serves 2

. . . .

1/2 pound fish fillet

3/4 cup nonfat cottage cheese

1/4–1/2 cup fine bread crumbs

1/2 cup fresh chopped mushrooms

1/2 pound fresh spinach

Preheat the oven to 350° F. Cut the fish into 1/4-inch or slightly thinner pieces. Cover the bottom of an oiled glass baking dish with the fish. Mix the cottage cheese, bread crumbs, and mushrooms, then spread over the fish to form a layer about 3/8-inch thick. Cover with spinach to prevent dehydration. Bake for 15 minutes, or until the fish appears done from under the baking dish; the fish will turn white and flake apart when tested with a fork. Pickles and steamed cauliflower florets make excellent accompaniments.

COD ITALIANO

Serves 4

Contrary to popular belief, olive oil and garlic are not obligatory for all Italian cuisine. For example, I have never had ice cream containing garlic. Even tomatoes are sometimes omitted, but not from baked codfish. A friend passed along this Old World information.

2 pounds cod fillets
1 medium onion, chopped
3 medium tomatoes
Olive oil

Preheat the oven to 350° F. Place the fish in an oiled glass baking dish and cover with the chopped onions and tomato. Sprinkle lightly with olive oil. Bake for 12 minutes or until fish flakes and appears done from below. Serve with garlic bread and pasta.

SEA LEG STUFFED POLLOCK

Serves 2 to 4

Although basically the same as a codfish, pollock does have a slightly different texture and flavor, which show up in this recipe.

INGREDIENTS

1–1-1/2 pound pollock fillets

4 ounces Ritz crackers

5-1/2 tablespoons butter or margarine

1-1/2 teaspoons lemon juice

2 tablespoons chopped fresh chives

2 sea leg sticks, finely chopped

A few spinach or lettuce leaves

PROCEDURE

Preheat the oven to 375° F. Slice the fillets 1/4 to 1/2 inch thick. Line an oiled glass baking dish with half the fish. Crumble the crackers into a bowl. Melt the 4 tablespoons of butter and mix in the lemon juice over low heat. Add to crackers along with chives. Stir in the sea legs. Of course fresh lobster or crab meat would be much better but the sea legs (highly compressed pollock processed with crab juices and red dye) are far less expensive. Cover the fish with the stuffing, then top stuffing with remaining fish. Cover with spinach or lettuce leaves to prevent browning, bake for 5 minutes. Take the dish from the oven and remove the leaves. Dot the fish with remaining butter and return to the oven for about 5 minutes more. The fish should be done but not completely browned. Run it under the broiler for a few seconds to achieve a brown top. Garnish with remaining chives and serve with green beans and sautéed onions.

CUSK COCKTAIL

Steam or poach the cusk fillets. Chill the cooked fillets, then place on lettuce leaves over a bed of ice. (Placing lettuce leaves between the fish and the melting ice keeps the fish from absorbing water and becoming soggy. This is a useful trick with shrimp or other seafood cocktails as well.) Serve with a seafood cocktail sauce and crispy crackers or toast squares as hors d'oeuvres and watch them disappear.

TERRY SHERRY COD

Serves 4

This is one of the finest ways of preparing fresh cod.

I N G R E D I E N T S

3 tablespoons butter or margarine, melted
Chopped fresh or dried tarrragon
2 pounds cod fillets

Splash of dry sherry
1-2 teaspoons lemon juice

P R O C E D U R E

Coat a heavy pan with vegatable oil spray or a little melted butter. Heat pan and sprinkle tarragon, then add the fish and saute until browned on one side, about 2 minutes. Turn over and sprinkle with sherry and saute on other side for an additional 2 minutes. When the fish is almost done, baste with melted butter and and lemon juice. Remove to a hot platter and reduce the liquid in the pan until slightly thickened. Pour the sauce over the fish and serve with garlic bread, green beans, and baked potatoes.

BIRTHDAY RICE

Serves 2

This dish was created for my wife's birthday but is equally delicious on all other days as well.

- 1 garlic clove, minced
- 1-1/2 tablespoons butter
- 1/2 pound cod fillets
- 1/2 pound cleaned medium shrimp
- 1/2 pound bay or small sea scallops
- 1 teaspoon rum
- 1 teaspoon chopped fresh tarragon leaves
- 3/4 cup rice, cooked

P R O C E D U R E

Sauté garlic in butter in a medium pan until soft, about 3 minutes. Chop the cod into pieces the size of the shrimp and scallops. Add the rum and tarragon to the butter sauce, then the fish and shellfish. Sauté until cooked through, about 2 minutes.

Arrange the rice on a plate and cover with fish mixture. Surround the fish with vegetable of choice and serve.

FISH CAKES

The mild-flavored cod, pollock, and haddock are all especially suitable for fish cakes. Here are two basic types.

BREAD CRUMB FISH CAKES

Serves 2

I N G R E D I E N T S

- 2 cups fine bread crumbs
- 1 small onion, chopped, or shallots

About 1 pound cod fillets

1/4 cup creamy salad dressing, or low-calorie mayonnaise

1 teaspoon lemon juice, or distilled white vinegar

1 teaspoon tamari (soy sauce)

2 medium eggs

1 tablespoon vegetable oil

P R O C E D U R E

Mix the bread crumbs and onion into a large mixing bowl. Flake the fillets carefully (always watch out for bones) into the bread mix. Add the remaining ingredients and mix well. Wipe a large iron skillet with a little oil and put it over a low heat, turning the pan to spread the oil all over the bottom. Drop the fish mixture by tablespoons into the pan and sauté until browned on both sides.

Note: If desired, bake these in the oven instead, on a lightly greased or sprayed cookie sheet. Form patties, dust with paprika (for added taste and appearance), and bake for 10 minutes.

TRADITIONAL FISH CAKES

Serves 4

Unlike Bread Crumb Fish Cakes, these traditional cakes use potato as the binding element. The result is a much heavier cake, usually flavored differently as well. In Boston, these are (or were) served with baked beans for Friday night supper. (Hallie Williams of Peru, Vermont, made the best baked beans I've ever tasted. She baked them slowly with maple syrup for a long time. The result was beyond anything. If anyone who reads this knows how to make beans that way, I humbly beseech their favor, please pass the recipe along.)

I N G R E D I E N T S

1 pound cod fillets

3 medium baked potatoes

1 small onion, very finely chopped

3 medium to large eggs or egg whites

Tamari (soy sauce) and/or lemon juice

1 tablespoon vegetable oil

P R O C E D U R E

Cook the fillets until they fall apart, about 12 minutes. Peel the potatoes and spoon the pulp into a large bowl. Add the fish and any liquid to the bowl along with the onions. Mix well, then add the eggs and mix thoroughly. Heat the oil in a large cast-iron skillet (the kind Grandma used to use distribute the heat evenly and do not impart teflon molecules into the food) over medium heat. When the oil is heated, add the mixture by tablespoons to the pan; it will form into silver-dollar-size pancakes. Cook until browned on one side, about 3 minutes, then brown the other side, another 3 minutes.

FISH
COOKERY

F O U R T E E N

FLOUNDER

From the tiny sand dab to the giant halibuts, flounders are superb eating. Size is the major deciding factor in how to cook these magnificent fish. Small fish are cooked whole to save all the meat possible, while mediums are filleted and large fish are steaks. Some restaurants batter coat and deep-fry the delicate fillets, thereby losing the fragile flavor. Breading and pan-frying work quite well if the chef is careful not to overcook the delicate fillets. Poaching, broiling, and baking are much easier and generally give better results. One profanity I hope never to see is deep-fried halibut—that would be heresy.

TERRE'S TREAT FLOUNDER

Serves 2 to 3

I N G R E D I E N T S

1-1/2 cups fine cornmeal (put regular-grind cornmeal through a blender and sift)

Herbs to taste (dill, tarragon)

1–2 pounds fresh flounder fillets

1–2 large eggs, lightly beaten

2–3 tablespoons bacon drippings

P R O C E D U R E

Season the cornmeal with herbs. Dip the fillets in beaten egg, then in the seasoned cornmeal. Heat bacon drippings in a skillet and add fish. Fry carefully (the fish is thin and cooks rapidly) until brown on one side, about 3 minutes, then flip and brown on the other side, about 3 minutes.

DEEP-FRIED FLOUNDER FILLETS

Deep-frying is a delicious way to prepare flounder; the fish tends to keep its moisture and remain flaky and crisp—if the process is done properly.

I N G R E D I E N T S

Vegetable oil (enough to fill pot 1/3 deep)

1/2 pound flounder fillets, per person

Batter of choice (pages 22–23)

In a large, heavy cast-iron pot, heat the oil to at least 375° F. Coat the fish in the batter. Drop fillets into it into the pot and fry a few at a time—or they will stick together—until brown, about 2 minutes. Drain in a single layer on paper towels or brown paper. Serve with Louisiana Red Sauce (page 68), commercial cocktail sauce, or Tartar Sauce (page 91).

MUSHROOM FLOUNDER

Serves 4

I N G R E D I E N T S

1–2 pounds fresh flounder fillets

1/2 cup sliced fresh mushrooms

1 10-ounce can condensed cream of mushroom soup, mixed with 1 tablespoon dry sherry

Paprika (optional)

Grated Pamesan cheese (optional)

2 tablespoons chopped shallots

2 tablespoons (1/4 stick) butter

1 cup small green peas, fresh if available

8 small Irish potatoes

P R O C E D U R E

Preheat the oven to 350° F. Lay the fillets in a single layer in an oiled glass baking dish. Put a layer of mushrooms on top and cover with the cream of mushroom soup mix. Sprinkle a little paprika or grated cheese on top for color. Bake for 30 minutes, or until fish flakes. Meanwhile, sauté the shallots in the butter for 2 minutes, then add the peas and simmer until the peas are done, about 3 minutes. Boil the potatoes until tender, about 10 minutes. Serve with fresh baked rolls.

POACHED FLOUNDER

Serves 4

INGREDIENTS

1–2 cups dry white wine mixed with water, as desired

1–2 pounds fresh flounder fillets

3 tablespoons chopped fresh parsley (optional)

PROCEDURE

In a wide pan large enough to hold the fillets in one layer, heat 1/4-inch of the poaching liquid to a boil. Put in the fish, cover, and cook until the fillets flake. Transfer the fillets to a hot platter and reduce liquid until thickened slightly, stirring constantly. Sprinkle in parsley and pour sauce over fillets. Serve with baked potatoes and fresh buttered asparagus.

SPUDDED FLOUNDER

Serves 4

For the fat-conscious, oven-frying is the greaseless way to "fry." A moist fish with a crispy crust can also be achieved this way.

INGREDIENTS

1–1-1/2 pounds fresh flounder fillets

2 large egg whites, lightly beaten, or 1 cup milk

1/2 cup instant potato flakes

Herbs as desired

2 tablespoons (1/4 stick) butter

3/4 teaspoon lemon juice

1 teaspoon dill seed

Preheat the oven to 350° F. Dip the fillets in the egg or milk and coat with the potato flakes and herbs. Arrange in a single layer in an oiled glass baking dish and drizzle with melted butter and lemon juice. Sprinkle a few dill seeds on the top. Bake for 10 minutes, then move the dish from the oven to broiler to brown, about 1 minute more. (This makes the fish crispy on the outside.) Serve with a vegetable and crisp French bread.

BROILED FLOUNDER

Serves 2 to 4.

Preparation doesn't come much simpler, or better.

I N G R E D I E N T S

2 tablespoons (1/4 stick)
butter or margarine

1 teaspoon lemon juice
1–2 pounds flounder fillets

P R O C E D U R E

Melt the butter in a small saucepan. Add the lemon juice and stir. Place the fillets in a broil pan, drizzle with the butter, and broil for 3 minutes. Serve with plain boiled new potatoes and French-style green beans.

FLOUNDER-STUFFED GRAPE LEAVES

Serves 4

Greek people gather young grape leaves in the summer and pack them in layers of salt to use later to stuff with a mixture of ground meat and rice. This is a variation on the idea, using fish. Preserved grape leaves can also be purchased in jars in specialty markets, or you can substitute boiled cabbage leaves. If using fresh grape leaves, soften them by soaking in hot water for one or two hours, or pickle them in brine for two weeks.

I N G R E D I E N T S

1 1/2 pounds flounder fillets

Herbs as desired (cumin, dill)

1 cup rice

20–24 grape leaves

1 10-ounce can condensed cream of mushroom soup mixed with 1/2 can water(optional)

P R O C E D U R E

Preheat the oven to 350° F. Steam the fillets until they flake, about 2 minutes. Boil the rice until tender, about 20 minutes. Mix fish and rice in a bowl and add remaining seasonings. Place a teaspoon of stuffing on a flattened grape leaf. Fold in the sides and roll up, tucking end under. Repeat with remaining grape leaves. Fill a pan with stuffed grape leaves, seam side down. Pour in soup mix to come about one-third to halfway up the stuffed leaves. Bake for 20 to 30 minutes, then serve hot with sauce.

Note: Adjust the seasoning if using cabbage leaves; for example, try caraway seeds in the filling.

SHRIMP-STUFFED FLOUNDER

Serves 4

Maine shrimp are available in certain seasons. They are not suitable for much more than stuffing; they are, however, very tasty.

1 tablespoon caraway seeds

3/4 pound small shrimp, peeled, deveined, and minced

1–1-1/2 pounds flounder fillets

2 tablespoons (1/4 stick) butter, melted

1 teaspoon lemon juice

P R O C E D U R E

Preheat the oven to 400° F. Sprinkle a few caraway seeds on the shrimp. Coat a flounder fillet with some shrimp and roll up. Skewer closed with a toothpick (use round picks). Repeat with remaining flounder and shrimp. Arrange rolls tightly in a glass baking dish and top with butter and lemon juice. Bake until fish flakes apart, about 5 minutes. Boiled dandelion greens and baked potatoes complete the menu.

BAKED STUFFED FLOUNDER

B ecause flounder is so mild, you can use virtually any stuffing to impart whatever flavor you would like. For example, you can use a classical chestnut stuffing as for a Christmas turkey, or a crab and bread crumb stuffing. A few suggestions follow.

WOLFFISH STUFFING

Makes enough for 4 servings

W hen I catch an ocean catfish (wolffish), it is usually too large to eat in a single meal and it does not freeze well, so we developed this lovely use for leftover baked wolffish, an especially good stuffing for flounder.

1 celery stalk (optional)

1 cup cooked wolffish

1/2 cup Ritz crackers

2 tablespoons (1/4 stick) butter, melted

1 teaspoon lemon juice

P R O C E D U R E

If you are using celery, soften in the microwave for 2 minutes on high. Mix ingredients in a bowl. Use to stuff fillets as for Shrimp-Stuffed Flounder (page 124).

CRAB MEAT STUFFING

Makes enough for 4 servings

Either real lump crab or sea legs (pressed pollock) works quite well. Crab tends to be juicier and requires less dry ingredients to achieve a good stuffing consistency. Parsley is a tasty addition for this stuffing.

I N G R E D I E N T S

3 tablespoons butter

1 cup lump crab meat or sea legs

Herbs as desired

3/4 cup bread crumbs

1/4 cup chopped fresh parsley

P R O C E D U R E

Melt the butter. Add the other ingredients and mix. Use to stuff fillets as for Shrimp-Stuffed Flounder (page 124).

Oyster Stuffing

Makes enough for 4 servings.

Oysters, because they have a distinctive flavor, do not appeal to all palates. Nevertheless, the wild rice makes this a fancy stuffing for company.

I N G R E D I E N T S

1 cup water
1/4 cup wild rice

1 cup diced cooked onion and green pepper
1 cup shucked oysters (1-1/2 dozen whole), with liquor

P R O C E D U R E

Bring water to a boil, add rice in a coverable pan, cover, and cook over low heat until water is absorbed by the rice and rice is tender, about 45 minutes.

Combine the rice, vegetables, and oysters in a bowl. Add enough oyster liquor to dampen the mix. Use to stuff fillets as for Shrimp-Stuffed Flounder (page 124).

Other Stuffings

Scallops, clams, mussels, and other shellfish make distinctive stuffings for flounder. And almonds or ham bits with cheese are also good. Also, consider leftover flounder as an excellent stuffing for other dishes.

Flounder Cordon Bleu

Serves 2

I N G R E D I E N T S

4–6 flounder fillets
4–6 thin slices Virginia ham

4—6 thin slices Swiss cheese

2 tablespoons (1/4 stick) butter, melted

1 teaspoon lemon juice

Paprika

Fresh parsley sprigs

P R O C E D U R E

Preheat the oven to 350° F. Lay a flounder fillet on the counter, cover with a slice of ham and a thin slice of cheese, then roll up the fillet with ham and cheese inside and close with a round toothpick. Repeat for remaining fillets. Pack fillets into a glass baking dish, drizzle butter and lemon over the top, sprinkle with paprika, and bake for 10 minutes, or until fish flakes. Garnish with parsley sprigs and serve with boiled new potatoes and spring peas.

F I F T E E N

MARINE PERCH

Marine perches come in three different colors: red, white, and blue. The red perch (rosefish, redfish, ocean perch) lives in deep, cold waters, but the other two overlap in the coastal waters and estuaries of New England. We do sometimes catch them jigging for codfish—usually on a pink plastic shrimp-tail teaser—but they are not a treat the average angler can plan on. They are available in the supermarket, but remember that a fish in the supermarket has probably been dead for at least five days before you buy it.

The blue perch (cunner, bergall, damned-bait-stealer) lives mostly from the tide line down and out to about five or six miles from the coast, although I have

129

caught large ones in the considerably deeper waters of Cashes Ledge and Georges Banks. These hungry little fish eat bait intended for other consumers. They are very good, but the ones that are commonly caught are too small to be conveniently cleaned for cooking. The fillets are quite small, so broiling or baking is not practical. Chowder is the usual destination. Larger bergalls can be treated exactly like small cod. The meat is tender, white, and mild, but it does not freeze well, so keep only enough for immediate consumption.

White perch (sea perch) spawns in the New England rivers from late March through May. It has been successfully established in many freshwater lakes. Basically a saltwater fish, it has adapted well to fresh water. These smaller cousins of the striped bass make their spring journey up the rivers to continue their kind. Early in their run the fish don't taste badly of the river, but this condition ceases rapidly. Consequently, immediate filleting and skinning are a fast rule.

There are many ways of preparing white perch, but fillets are usually first marinated in lemon juice, salad dressing, pickle juice, wine, or other liquid to enhance flavor.

Often I cut the fillets into 1/4-inch wide strips before marinating. These fingers are excellent rolled in seasoned bread crumbs and baked or broiled. Another method is to roll them in flour, dip them in milk, then roll them in seasoned bread crumbs and deep-fry. You may also like to try poaching them in the same manner as the yellow perch (page 177).

DILLY REDFISH

Serves 4

Preparation of these little fish is very simple, although if dealing with a whole fish be extremely careful. The dorsal and gill plate cover spines carry a toxin that can make you quite remorseful. Wear a pair of kevlar fish cleaning gloves for safety. If you do get spined, see a doctor; the toxin is not a joke. There are also lateral line bones, as in scup or black sea bass, which must be removed for eating comfort.

2 pounds red perch fillets

3 tablespoons butter

Fresh dill or chives

P R O C E D U R E
. . . .

Sauté the fillets in butter along with fresh dill or chives until fish flakes, about 2 minutes.

WHITE PERCH CASSEROLE

Serves 3

I N G R E D I E N T S
. . . .

3/4 cup chopped celery	2 teaspoons Dijon mustard
1/2 cup chopped onion	Pinch of pepper
1 chicken bouillon cube	1 tablespoon chopped fresh parsley
1 tablespoon butter	2 cups diced mixed cooked vegetables
1/4 cup olive oil	1-1/2 cups flaked cooked white perch fillets
2 teaspoons cornstarch	Seasoned bread crumbs
1 cup milk	Grated Parmesan cheese

P R O C E D U R E
. . . .

Preheat the oven to 350° F. Place celery, onion, bouillon cube, butter, and oil in a microwaveable dish. Cover with perforated plastic wrap or a paper towel to prevent splattering and microwave on high for about 4 minutes, or until onion and celery are soft.

Combine cornstarch and milk in a medium saucepan. Add onion mixture and mustard, pepper, and parsley. Cook over medium heat, stirring constantly until thickened, about 5 minutes. Add vegetables to the sauce. Stir in fish. Pour into medium baking dish, sprinkle with bread crumbs and cheese, and bake for about 20 minutes or until casserole is bubbly. Stir and serve with garlic bread.

WHITE PERCH A L'ORANGE

Serves 4

Because white perch is relatively strong-flavored, heavier seasonings such as orange juice, soy sauce, cumin, mustard, and wine are welcome.

I N G R E D I E N T S

- 2 cups orange juice
- 2 tablespoons soy sauce
- 2 teaspoons minced garlic
- 1-1/2 teaspoons ground cumin or chili powder
- 1-1/2–2 pounds white perch fillets

P R O C E D U R E

Combine first 4 ingredients and marinate the fillets for 2 to 12 hours in refrigerator. Preheat the broiler. Drain fillets and place in broil pan. Broil until fish flakes, about 20 minutes.

WHITE PERCH DIJON

Serves 4

I N G R E D I E N T S

- 2 pounds white perch fillets
- 2 tablespoons Dijon mustard
- 1 cup dry white wine

132

P R O C E D U R E

Preheat the broiler. Place fillets in a broil pan and broil for 5 minutes. Combine the mustard and wine. Remove the fish from the broiler and cover it with the mixture. Return to broiler and finish cooking until fish flakes, about 3 minutes. Serve with lima beans and dinner rolls.

JAMAICAN JERK PERCH

Serves 4

J erk spice, a blend of herbs from Jamaica, is sprinkled over fillets that are then broiled. It's hot and good.

I N G R E D I E N T S

1/4 cup lemon juice

1 quart water

1–2 pounds skinless perch fillets

3 tablespoons butter or margarine

Jerk spices (see page 26)

P R O C E D U R E

Mix the lemon juice and water, then marinate the fillets for about 30 minutes. Preheat the broiler. Drain and pat the fish dry. Place the fish in a single layer in a clear glass baking dish. Dot with butter or margarine and sprinkle with the spices. Broil the fish until it flakes, about 4 minutes. Accompany with corn on the cob and baked potatoes.

WARM SEAS FINFISH

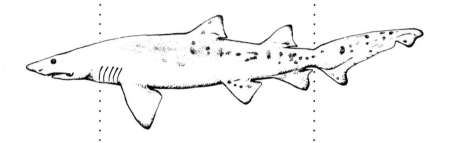

S I X T E E N

FLORIDA FISH

M ost of the warm seas fish are relatively highly flavored. Those that are not are usually cooked in more highly spiced dishes. Jamaican jerk spices work exceptionally well on these fish—just dot the fish fillets with butter, sprinkle on some of the spices, and broil. Strong fish are also excellent prepared Cracker style (page 25). If you wish to prepare the fish a bit less agressively, soak it in a lime water solution (juice of two limes to a gallon of water) for about 30 minutes before cooking. Most restaurants seem to prefer deep-frying; few do it well.

In this chapter, I discuss first some common smaller seafood caught in the southeastern U.S. waters, then discuss particularly popular types like shark and tuna, and conclude with the more exotic varieties.

Florida vacations have yielded some interesting close encounters of the fourth kind (i.e., assimilation).

In general it is well to note that warm-water fish tend to have much stronger tastes than their cooler relatives, so we compensate—usually with seasonings.

Snappers and groupers. The various snappers and groupers are the commonest of Florida fish. They are the warm-water equivalent of cod and can be treated much the same way, except that their flavor is generally stronger. Fresh broiled grouper is a treat, but deep-fried is much more likely to be encountered in Florida restaurants. Snappers contain an oil that prevents them from freezing well, but this same feature makes them well suited for fish chowders and baked dishes. Red snapper seems to be the one exception with respect to flavor; the meat is excellent stuffed and baked simply.

Black Drum. Under the bridges between Tampa and St. Petersburg swim some of the largest fish you will encounter fishing from shore, at least in the continental United States. Tarpon over a hundred pounds and black drum nearly half that size are common. Fly fishermen love to wrestle the enormous bony tarpon. Bait fishermen angle for such prize-eating fish as pompano, cobia, and summer flounder. Black drum are not to be sneezed at. True, the large ones tend to have huge round worms lying along their backbones, but these are easily excised, leaving plenty of delicious meat. (Don't worry if you miss a worm or two; they can't hurt you). There are, no doubt, many ways to prepare the fish, but I have delicious results when I simply cut the meat into 3/4-inch cubes, dip them in a beer batter, and deep-fry them. Pompano and cobia are both good broiling fish, while summer flounder can be treated the same as flounder caught in northern waters.

Amberjack. Fish markets in Florida frequently market amberjack meat as tuna, the implication being that it can be treated the same way. I can't say from personal experience, but there are many tuna recipes (Chapter 18). The first time I caught an amberjack was on an overnight party-boat trip in the Gulf of Mexico. The mates conned me into believing that the fish was not worth the effort and I gave it to them. The lesson was: If someone says a fish is inedible, don't just give it to him. Ask at least three other people. If they agree, throw the fish back. If they disagree but express reservations (bones, possible toxin) either try to deal with the fish, release it, or give it to the least negative person. There are unscrupulous people in any business, but the mates on most fishing boats are honest, helpful, and dependent on tips for a living. I later learned that amberjack steaks are excellent broiled with lemon butter or pan-fried.

Wreckfish. If you see a fish that looks like an enormous black and gray angelfish, chances are it is a wreckfish. These are good eating, but they tend to a strong flavor common to all Florida fishes. They are thin enough so that techniques such as poaching or grilling are best.

Triggerfish. Offshore trips to the reefs in the center of the Gulf of Mexico frequently yield these rather strange-looking creatures, as does surface fishing in the upper Keys during the day. The meat is good and adapts well to broiling, baking, or frying. The skin of these fish is the toughest to cut through I have yet encountered, so use a sharp knife to clean them. Most party boat skippers will tell you to throw them out, largely because they are so hard to clean. But since you usually catch these dogged fighters when you are after the much-more-desired yellowtail snapper, it is not surprising that these tasty fish are usually not kept.

Porgies. Although these fish come in many colors, they are the warm-water version of scup. Their flavor is somewhat stronger than their northern cousins, so freshening them with a lime water marinade is an excellent idea. Follow the recipe on page 96.

Clams. These are mostly the same as their New England relatives except that they have a stronger flavor. The razor clam is better for chowder, since the hard-shell (quahog) clams are usually very large and tough. Natives prefer the tiny cocinas or penshell clams. Calicos are another good chowder clam; their stronger flavor makes them much less desirable for such dishes as clams casino or stuffed clams.

Florida Snail. There are a wide variety of large edible snails, which can be treated as conchs (see page 85.)

Florida Oysters. Everywhere you walk along the canals are razor-sharp oyster shells (I have the scars to prove it). Here the problem is to pick them from clean, well-irrigated waters. They are delicious and virtually indistinguishable from their Northern counterparts, except that you must be very careful where you pick them. The warmer waters allow harmful bacteria to propagate much more rapidly than the cold North Atlantic waters.

Florida cats. These suffer from a solial stigma. Most natives look down their noses at these prolific scavengers; yet the meat is good. Frequently the large ones are infected with worms. Cut these out if necessary, and grind the meat to tenderize it, to make delicious fish cakes or chowder.

Southern mackerel. The Spanish, or king, mackerel are entirely different from the tinkers of Yankee waters. The meat is much milder than that of their northern relatives, and they are also much larger. Fillet and skin these warm-water pisces.

Honey-Dijon Spanish Mackerel

Serves 4

INGREDIENTS

2 pounds mackerel fillets

2 tablespoons Dijon mustard

1 cup honey

PROCEDURE

Preheat the broiler or prepare grill. Broil or grill the fillets for about 5 minutes. Mix the mustard and honey and liberally coat the half-cooked fillets. Return fish to the heat and finish cooking until the fish flakes, another 4–5 minutes. Collard greens and black-eyed peas have enough character to go well with this dish.

Poached Spanish Mackerel

Serves 4

INGREDIENTS

Dry white wine, water, or other poaching liquid

2 pounds mackerel fillets

PROCEDURE

Pour enough poaching liquid into a large pot to come to about 1/2-inch depth. Bring to a boil, then put the fillets in, remove pot from heat, and cover immediately. The fish cooks in the hot liquid in about 10 minutes. Drain and serve with linguine and snow peas.

BAKED SPANISH MACKEREL

Serves 4

I N G R E D I E N T S

2 pounds mackerel fillets

1 cup crushed Ritz crackers

2 tablespoons (1/4 stick) butter, melted

2 tablespoons chopped fresh chives

1 tablespoon chopped fresh dill

Juice of 1/4 lime or 1/2 lemon

Lettuce leaves, cucumber and tomoto slices, for serving
Dill weed

P R O C E D U R E

Preheat the oven to 350° F. Place fillets in an oiled glass baking dish in a single layer. In a bowl, mix the cracker crumbs, butter, chives, dill, and lemon or lime juice. Spread over the fillets and bake for 10–12 minutes, or until fish turns white as seen from underneath. Run the dish under the broiler to brown the dressing. Cover a platter with lettuce leaves and place the cooked fish in the middle. Surround with slices of cucumber and tomato. Serve with plain boiled rice.

JERKED MACKEREL

Serves 4

I N G R E D I E N T S

2 pounds mackerel fillets

Jerk spices

1 tablespoon butter

Preheat the broiler. Arrange the fillets in a single layer in an oiled clear glass baking dish. Sprinkle with spices and dot with butter. Broil the fish until it flakes easily, about 6 minutes.

CRACKER MACKEREL

Serves 4

This is a great way to cook fish outdoors on a grill, although there is nothing (except the possibility of spilling and making a mess) the matter with doing it in an oven. The delicate flavor of the Southern fish makes it a fortuitous choice.

I N G R E D I E N T S

2 *pounds mackerel fillets*
1 *tablespoon butter*
2 *grapefruits*

P R O C E D U R E

Prepare a charcoal grill. Lay the fillets individually on a sheet of aluminum foil and dot with butter. Squeeze the juice of half of a grapefruit over each piece of fish. Pull the foil up around the fish to hold the juice and crimp the edges so steam will be retained. Grill the packages outside until the fish flakes freely (check doneness by opening the packages and peeking at the fish every couple of minutes), about 5 minutes. The combination of fish and grapefruit juices, cooked together, makes a sauce that you'll have to taste to believe. Serve with green beans and potatoes (recipe follows).

Green Beans and Potatoes

Serves 4

I N G R E D I E N T S

1 pound fresh green beans

3 strips lean bacon

3 medium potatoes

P R O C E D U R E

Wash and snap ends off the beans. Break the beans into pieces 1 to 2 inches long. Place the beans in a pot with enough water to cover. Cut the bacon into pieces about an inch long and add them to the pot. Simmer for about half an hour. Cut the potatoes into quarters while the beans simmer. Add the potatoes and continue simmering until the potatoes are done and the water is reduced by three-fourths, about 25 minutes.

Seafood Lasagna

Each dish serves 8

The oils of Florida fish make them especially suited to this dish.

Lasagna is one of those dishes that cannot be properly made in small quantities, so the ingredients are *doubled*.

I N G R E D I E N T S

1/4 cup plus 1 tablespoon olive oil

2 garlic cloves

2 cups minced onions

2 32-ounce jars of spaghetti sauce

1 tablespoon chopped fresh basil

3/4 pound lasagna noodles

12 ounces cottage cheese

4 ounces mozzarella cheese, crumbled

8 ounces parmesan cheese, grated

1 pound cleaned shrimp

1 pound snapper fillets

P R O C E D U R E

Preheat oven the to 350° F. In a large pot, put the 1/4 cup olive oil and garlic. Sauté the garlic until it browns, about 2 minutes, then crush to extract flavor into the oil. Discard the garlic and put in the onions. Sauté until softened, about 3 minutes. Add the spaghetti sauce and basil, turn heat to low, and simmer to blend the flavors. Cook the lasagna noodles according to package directions, adding the remaining tablespoon of olive oil to the cooking water. Drain the noodles and separate them on wax paper. Blend the cheeses. Chop and mix the shrimp and fish. Layer each bottom of two 9 × 13-inch baking dishes with a thin layer of spaghetti sauce, a layer of noodles, a layer of seafood mix, then a layer of cheese. Repeat to use up the ingredients, ending with a layer of spaghetti sauce. Bake for about 40 minutes, then let lasagna cool for about 10–15 minutes (if you can wait that long). Unless you're feeding a dozen or more people, freeze one dish after cooling it to room temperature. (Cover the top of the dish with freezer wrap to prevent freezer burn.) Serve with garlic bread and antipasto salad.

SEVENTEEN

SHARKS, SKATES, AND RAYS

There are a vast number of sharks, ranging from the great white of *Jaws* fame to the lowly dogfish of coastal New England. Popular mythology notwithstanding, sharks generally are retiring and harmless—two hundred years document only one true shark attack in the Northeast. Of course, to deliberately provoke reaction by chumming or trying to boat one of these well-armored creatures is not the safest activity; a friend, knowing better than to get anywhere near the biting end, had his boat trashed by a supposedly dead thresher's tail.

Most sharks are good to eat, usually tasting rather like swordfish, but they require special care because of their peculiar biology. Modern fish regulate osmotic* pressure by a kidney, but sharks are primitive and carry uric acid in their blood for osmotic balance. The acid breaks down very quickly after the fish dies, releasing ammonia into the blood. So sharks must be bled and eviscerated at once if they are to be eaten.

A note of interest is that the upper part (lobe) of a shark's tail is much larger than the lower, so if you see a dorsal fin followed by an oscillating tail tip, it is probably a shark. The fish have no swim bladder (the main up-and-down mechanism for most fish), so they regulate vertical position by oversized pectoral fins, which push up, and the oversized upper tail lobe, which pushes down.

The following recipes are, by no means, the only ways to prepare shark. One day when only dogfish (sand sharks) were biting, the skipper of our party boat came around with a huge tray of delicious white meat. After everyone had sampled and acclaimed the fish, he revealed that it was broiled dogfish. (The percentage of fish returned to the water declined markedly.) The English prize dogfish with chips (French fries). Shark meat is versatile, tasty, and an excellent source of protein with *no bones*. Only unreasoned prejudice has kept shark meat from the culinary attention it deserves.

Should you be the lucky fisherman who catches a mako (one of the mackerel sharks), waste no time. Cut that prize into steaks and cook as for your favorite swordfish recipe. You can freeze whatever is left over. The sand shark (usually caught by surf-casting with bait) is edible, but you have to be hungry. Cut the skinned pieces into 1-inch widths so they don't curl up in the frying pan. Blue shark has a flavor very like the mako, but prompt cleaning is especially necessary. Steak the fish, then skin before broiling. I prefer to soak the steaks in a solution of 1/4 cup lemon juice to 1 gallon of water for at least 20 minutes to freshen even the freshest blue shark.

The Florida Department of Natural Resources has several publications containing shark recipes for such varied applications as soup, salad, baked shark, oven-fried shark, deep-fried shark, and shark casseroles. There are even people who fish for black-fin sharks commercially along the Florida coast. Floridians suggest soaking the fillets in a solution of ice water and salt (one cup salt to one gallon of water) for two hours to whiten the flesh and neutralize any residual ammonia. To cook shark for use in a recipe, cut the meat into 1/2-inch-thick slices and spread out on a microwave-safe dish. Microwave on high for 2 minutes; the meat is done when it flakes apart with a fork.

---

* Osmosis—divide a container into two parts by a semi-permeable membrane. Fill both parts with pure water. Now add salt to just one part. In a while the salt will migrate through the membrane until both sides are equally salty. The process is called osmosis. If a fish's blood is more or less salty than the surrounding water, some kind of pump is needed to counteract osmosis; modern fish accomplish this with kidneys, while sharks balance external pressure by blood inclusion (uric acid).

FISH
COOKERY

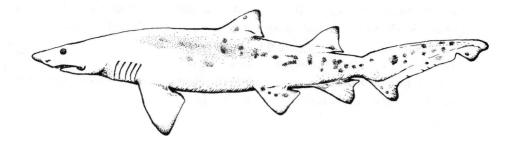

SHARK CASSEROLE

Serves 3

INGREDIENTS

3/4 cup chopped celery

1/2 cup chopped onion

1 chicken bouillon cube

1/4 cup (1/2 stick) butter or margarine

2 teaspoons cornstarch

1 cup whole milk

2 cups chopped mixed vegetables (see note)

1 tablespoon chopped fresh parsley

Pinch of pepper

1 cup chopped cooked shark meat

1 package refrigerator rolls

PROCEDURE

Preheat the oven to 350° F. Place celery, onion, bouillon cube, and butter in a microwave-safe dish. Cover with perforated plastic wrap or a paper towel to prevent splattering, and microwave on high for about 2 minutes or until onion and celery are soft; or sauté them on the top of stove.

Combine the cornstarch and milk in a medium saucepan. Add the vegetables, parsley, and pepper. Cook over medium heat, stirring constantly, to thicken sauce, about 10 minutes.

147

Stir the onion mixture and flaked fish into the sauce. Pour into a medium baking dish. Break apart rolls and put on top of the casserole. Bake for about 20 minutes, or until the casserole is golden brown and bubbly.

Note: You can precook the vegetables with a pat of butter in a microwave for a couple of minutes if you desire, or add them raw to the sauce. Frozen vegetables should be thawed before adding them to the sauce.

BAKED SHARK

Serves 2 or 3

I N G R E D I E N T S

1/4 cup lemon juice

1 gallon water

1 pound piece of shark fillet or steak

3–4 slices bacon

1/2 cup thinly sliced onions

3–5 teaspoons minced fresh parsley

A few drops of dry sherry

1/4–1/2 cup soft bread crumbs

P R O C E D U R E

Preheat the oven to 350° F. Make a freshening marinade of the lemon juice and water. Place the fish in the marinade and let soak for 20 to 30 minutes.

Fry bacon until crisp, about 5 minutes. Drain on paper towels and crumble. Sauté the onion in the bacon drippings until soft, about 3 minutes. Take the pan off the heat and add the parsley and bacon.

Spread the fish in an 8-inch oiled baking dish. Sprinkle with sherry, then cover fish evenly with the bacon mixture. Sprinkle the bread crumbs over the top and bake for 25 to 30 minutes or until the fish flakes on fork testing.

BAKED SHARK WITH VEGETABLES

Serves 2

INGREDIENTS

2 cups fresh or frozen chopped
   mixed vegetables (see note)

3/4–1 pound shark fillets

1/4 cup finely chopped red onion

1-1/2 tablespoons margarine

1 tablespoon all-purpose flour

3/4 cup water

1/2 teaspoon tamari (soy sauce)

Bread crumbs and chopped fresh parsley

PROCEDURE

Preheat the oven to 350° F. Sauté the onions in half the margarine until soft, about 3 minutes. In a heavy skillet, make a paste of the remaining butter and the flour. Add the onion and slowly stir in the water and soy sauce, stirring constantly. Reduce mixture slightly to make an onion gravy. Put the fish in a single layer in a well-oiled baking dish. Combine the vegetables and gravy, then spread over the fish. Garnish with bread crumbs or parsley. Cover and bake for 25 to 30 minutes, or until the fish flakes when tested with a fork.

Note: Frozen vegetables can be quickly thawed by spreading in a half-inch layer in a microwave oven and cooking at high heat for about 2 minutes.

EASY SHARK SOUP

Serves 4

INGREDIENTS

1/2 cup chopped onion

1/4 cup (1/2 stick) margarine

3 tablespoons dry sherry

1 quart half-and-half

1 can condensed cream of
    shrimp soup
1/2 cup all-purpose flour
1 teaspoon grated lemon peel

1 teaspoon paprika
2 pounds flaked cooked shark meat
3 hard-boiled egg yolks, finely chopped
Chopped fresh parsley, for garnish

P R O C E D U R E

Sauté the onion in margarine until soft but not brown, about 3 minutes. Gradually add the soup, flour, lemon peel, and paprika, stirring constantly. Stir in the sherry and the half-and-half, then simmer over medium heat until reduced slightly. While stirring add the fish and egg yolks. When the soup is heated through, garnish with parsley.

SHARK HORS D'OEUVRES

Serves 2

I N G R E D I E N T S

6 ounces cream cheese, at room temperature
1 cup flaked cooked shark meat
3 tablespoons margarine, at room temperature
3 tablespoons salad dressing
2 tablespoons chopped chives or scallions
Sesame crackers or wheat thins
Grated cheese

P R O C E D U R E

Place the softened cream cheese in a mixing bowl, and add the shark meat, margarine, salad dressing, and chives or scallions. Mix well. Spread on crackers, dust with cheese, and broil until lightly browned, about 3 minutes.

SHARK À L'ORANGE

Serves 2

I N G R E D I E N T S

1 pound shark fillets

Orange juice

4 tablespoons (1/2 stick) margarine, melted

Parsley sprigs and orange slices, for garnish

P R O C E D U R E

Marinate the fillets in orange juice to cover for several hours in refrigerator. Preheat the broiler. Arrange fillets in a shallow glass baking dish. Pour margarine over fish and broil for 3 minutes. Turn the fish and baste with butter sauce, then finish cooking, about another 3 minutes or until fish flakes. Garnish and serve.

BATTER-FRIED SHARK

Serves 4 to 6

I N G R E D I E N T S

Vegetable oil, for deep-frying

2 pounds shark fillets

2 cups Beer Batter (page 22)

P R O C E D U R E

Heat the oil to 425–450° F. Cut fillets into 1-inch cubes. Dip fish in batter and drop the cubes into the hot oil. When the pieces are browned, in about 3 minutes, they are ready. Spread the hot cubes on paper towels to drain.

SKATES AND RAYS

Think of these fish as flattened sharks, just as flounders are flattened bony fish. The principal difference is that the tail, not the head, is the dangerous end, although the powerful wings of a manta ray are quite capable of smashing a small boat.

My personal dining acquaintance has been only with the small and barn door skates of the Northeast Atlantic coast. But a friend from the Florida Keys says that the rays are second in taste only to yellowtail snappers. They are prepared in the same manner as any other mild-flavored fish. Indeed, since the quality of a fish's flesh reflects its diet, other skates and rays should be just fine.

When I celebrated my twenty-first birthday at a fancy restaurant in Denver, Colorado, the menu read "fresh sea scallops, flown in from the coast." They were no doubt from the coast, but they sure weren't scallops. Scallops have fibers running perpendicular to the circular faces; these "scallops" had fibers parallel to the faces. Skate wings cut with a circular punch have striations parallel to the round faces. Enough said? This remains a common practice.

Texture and taste differ slightly, but skate scallops are really a pretty good substitute. There are only two major problems. First, skate has a cartilaginous mass that runs through the wings, parallel to the faces. Second, the flavor of skate is much more delicate and will be lost if you try to do anything but lightly sauté it in butter. If the skate is large enough, cut the cartilage out and use a sharp cutter to get decent-size psuedoscallops. The flavor is somewhere between lobster and crab—excellent, but requiring a very light touch. Anything more than butter will mask the taste.

FISH
COOKERY

E I G H T E E N

TUNA

All tuna is good, but some species are better prepared one way while others are better done another way. The common tunas of the East Coast are bluefin, bigeye, yellowfin, albacore, false albacore (fat albert), and bonita. Japanese buyers wait at the dock—and even in off-shore boats—to buy the large bluefin and bigeye tuna, sometimes bidding to prices we consider astronomical. (In 1987, one Rhode Island fisherman received $28 a pound for his quarter-ton fish.) Smaller bluefin and yellowfin are the bulk of New England commercial tuna, bringing less than one-tenth of the per-pound price of large bluefins and bigeyes. Yellowfins keep well, freeze well. and are excellent for cooking and canning. The other tunas do not keep well and are totally ignored commercially in the Northeast Atlantic. This is a shame because albacore is the best eating of all, either fresh or canned. But albacore will not freeze well, making canning a necessity. (There is no cannery on the East Coast.) False albacore and bonita are smaller fish, but also good eating. They, too, do not freeze well and their meat is too soft for canning. Generally only small bluefin and yellowfin are marketed in the East.

Frozen tuna keeps well if the fish is frozen in water; otherwise, the fish will keep only for a couple of months. We developed the following recipe with tuna that had been frozen for about seven months—much longer than tuna frozen without ice could possibly be kept. The tuna should be frozen in fairly large loin pieces. We freeze ours in four-steak portions. Small bluefin or yellowfin freeze well.

Canning tuna is discussed here in considerable detail. Follow the directions *exactly*. Deviation from USDA recommended procedures can be fatal.

TUNA STEAKS FROM THE FREEZER

Serves 4

INGREDIENTS

4 large frozen tuna steaks
3 tablespoons lemon juice
2 tablespoons fresh tarragon
1 quart water
2 tablespoons (1/4 stick) butter
Dijon mustard

PROCEDURE

Take frozen tuna from freezer and thaw in refrigerator overnight. About 2 hours before you want to cook it, slice it into steaks and place in a glass dish with 2-inch sides. Add 2 tablespoons lemon juice to water and pour the marinade over the fish. Let sit for about 2 hours to draw out any residual blood and freezer flavors.

Preheat the broiler. Lay fish steaks on a baking platter. Add tarragon and remaining lemon juice to butter and pour over the fish. Broil the fish until brown on one side, about 5 minutes; turn and baste other side with butter that has run off into the pan. Broil on the second side until brown, about 5 minutes. Spread mustard on top and serve.

SKIPPER'S
YELLOWFIN OR BLUEFIN

Serves 4

S everal tuna boat captains and mates of my acquaintance claim this is the best way to eat tuna. Dip fresh yellowfin or bluefin steaks in French dressing and grill until they flake, about 10 minutes.

TUNA STEAKS
SAUTÉED WITH GARLIC

Serves 4

I N G R E D I E N T S

1 garlic clove

2 tablespoons (1/4 stick) butter or margarine

2 tablespoons olive oil

2 tablespoons chopped fresh tarragon

1 tablespoon chopped fresh oregano

4 fresh tuna steaks (yellowfin, albacore, false albacore, or bonita)

Sauté the garlic in the butter and oil until soft, about 3 minutes. Add the herbs and tuna, then sauté the tuna on both sides until it flakes apart, about 10 minutes. Serve with rice and tossed salad.

BLUEFIN STEAKS SAUTÉED WITH ONIONS

Serves 4

I N G R E D I E N T S
. . . .

2 medium onions, chopped

2 tablespoons (1/4 stick) butter or margarine

2 tablespoons olive oil

Pinch of fresh dill

Pinch of minced fresh basil

4 fresh bluefin steaks

1-1/2 teaspoons soy sauce

1 tablespoon dry sherry

P R O C E D U R E
. . . .

Sauté the onions in the olive oil and butter or margarine until translucent, about 2 minutes. Remove from the pan and add herbs and fish, then the soy sauce and sherry. Cook until the fish is mostly done, about 7 minutes. Return onions to the pan and finish cooking the onions and fish, another 3 minutes. Serve with a three-bean salad and toasted French bread.

BLUEFIN STEAKS SAUTÉED WITH ONIONS II

Serves 4

I N G R E D I E N T S
. . . .

2 medium onions, chopped

Drippings from 2–3 strips bacon

4 fresh tuna steaks

Sauté the onions in the bacon drippings until three-quarters done, about 2 minutes, then remove and set aside. Add the tuna and brown on one side for 5 minutes, then turn and cover with the onions. Continue cooking until the tuna is done, another 5 minutes.

ALBACORE STEAKS WITH DILL

Serves 4

Simple but elegant.

INGREDIENTS

4 albacore steaks
1 lime
2 tablespoons (1/4 stick) butter

Sprinkling of dry sherry
Chopped fresh dill
Garlic powder

PROCEDURE

Preheat the broiler. Lay steaks in a broil pan, squeeze lime over them, and dot with butter. Broil until lightly brown, about 5 minutes, then turn and sprinkle with sherry, dill, and garlic powder. Broil on the second side until the meat flakes with a fork, about 5 minutes.

157

TUNA ULTIMA

Serves 2

INGREDIENTS

1/4 cup chopped broccoli florets

1/4 cup sliced fresh mushrooms

1 small onion

3 teaspoons butter

2 fresh tuna steaks

Juice of 1/4 lime

2 fresh medium tomatoes

2 tablespoons chopped fresh dill

1 tablespoon fresh tarragon

Dry sherry

2 onion bagels

Garlic powder

PROCEDURE

Preheat the broiler. Steam the broccoli florets until tender, about 10 minutes. Sauté the mushrooms and the onion in butter until soft, about 3 minutes. Place the tuna steaks in an oiled glass baking dish, dot with butter, and squeeze lime juice over them. Broil fish for 5 minutes. While fish cook, cut the fresh tomatoes into small pieces. Place broccoli in a glass bowl and add the mushroom mix and tomato pieces. Sprinkle liberally with dill and stir. Turn the fish and sprinkle with tarragon and sherry, then return to heat to cook for additional 5 minutes.

Split the bagels, then butter and sprinkle with garlic powder. Warm in the oven. Remove fish from broiler and place on serving plates. Surround with the broccoli salad and serve with bagels.

SASHIMI

Last summer a group of about thirty of us were offshore fishing for tuna, having indifferent success. There were only a half-dozen small bluefin aboard when we reluctantly turned toward home. The mates began cleaning, finished the first fish, and prepared to dump the carcass overboard. Suddenly someone held up a bottle of soy sauce and shouted, "Wait! Don't throw it over!" He took the carcass to a nearby bench and nine people appeared, virtually out of nowhere. In less than ten minutes only bare bones remained. The little pieces of meat we pulled off the rack were delicious with just soy sauce but would have been better with the traditional Japanese sashimi sauce.

The friends who brought this recipe back from a stay in Japan say that sashimi is as close to a national dish as exists there. The Japanese use the basic sauce as a dip for raw slices of tuna, mackerel, or bluefish. The sauce with the optional olive oil becomes a garnish for chicken and other dishes.

I N G R E D I E N T S

3 teaspoons dry mustard
2 tablespoons soy sauce
1 tablespoon vinegar

2 tablespoons chicken broth
  (or bouillon dissolved in water)
Olive or oriental sesame oil (optional)
Pinch of sugar (optional)

P R O C E D U R E

Mix the mustard and soy sauce until mustard is dissolved. Add the vinegar, broth, and oil, if desired, and sweeten with sugar if you wish. Use to dip fish cut in 1/16-inch-thick pieces and serve with crackers and vegetable sticks.

Note: For bluefish or mackerel sashimi, freeze the fish for about 4 weeks to kill most of the bacteria of inshore waters. Slice and serve still partially frozen.

CANNING TUNA

If you are ever lucky enough to catch a tuna, be it bluefin, yellowfin, or albacore, you'll probably have more meat than you'll be able to eat before it spoils. Smoked tuna is delicious, but you can eat only so much. Frozen tuna keeps well if the fish is frozen in a block of ice. Fresh tuna only lasts about three days. To utilize all the meat, the answer is canning.

To can, cut out the dark meat and discard. Bleach the remaining meat overnight in a mixture of noniodized salt and ice, then follow either of the following procedures.

1. As recommended by the U.S. Department of Agriculture, steam the fish until done. Chill for 6 to 12 hours, then pack in hot canning jars with 3/4 to 1-inch head space. Add 1 to 2 teaspoons liquid to each pint, or 1/2 pint and a 1/2 teaspoon noniodized salt. Cap the jars and process in a pressure canner for 100 minutes at 10 pounds pressure. Cool and store in a cool, dark place.

2. Pack the bleached raw tuna in hot half-pint canning jars, then add 1-1/2 teaspoons olive oil and 1/2 teaspoon noniodized salt. Cap the jars loosely, bring to a boil in a pressure canner, tighten the rings, and process at 10 pounds pressure for 1 hour 40 minutes. Cool and store as above.

You may want to add herbs (dill, tarragon) to the fish when you can it, but do so with care. Processing at high temperatures for long periods emphasizes the characteristics of the herbs.

Home-canned tuna is far superior to what you buy in the grocery store, but be careful. If a jar does not seal, do not use the product. *Clostridium botulinum* does not forgive.

Smoked Tuna

Any tuna can be smoked, but albacore is so good canned or fresh that I fix it no other way. Yellowfin smokes well with a simple salt-(noniodized)-and-water marinade for about 2 hours, smoked with maple wood. Bluefin is best honey-mesquite smoked. For honey-mesquite smoking, make a marinade of 1 part honey to 4 parts hot water. Let the water cool slightly, then place the fish in it for about 3 hours (longer immersion gives a sweeter fish). Smoke gently over mesquite chips.

The choice of wood is extremely important in any smoking; hickory or apple work well for meats, but do not always give good results for fish. Bluefish, for example, sometimes acquires a very bitter aftertaste when smoked with apple wood. Woods that have a high sugar content usually give the best results for fish.

NINETEEN

SOME

OCEAN EXOTICS

Excellent eating is to be had with the less-known oceanic fishes.

Butterfish. Today butterfish are primarily marketed frozen as bait for tuna and shark fishing, but in prior years these fat, oily fish were prized. According to written reports as recent as 1945, these are "one of our best table fish."

Unfortunately, I can find no information as to how they have been prepared— nor, for that matter, any fresh fish to experiment with. My guess is that you treat them the same as tinker mackerel. They probably would be excellent smoked as

161

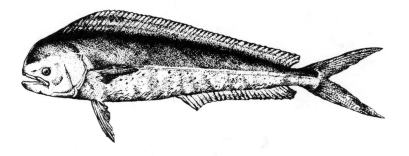

well, since they are oily. This same oiliness, incidentally, is what makes them such good bait. The oil dissolves in the water and acts as chum—a dinner bell for itinerate pisces.

Dolphin (mahi-mahi). A woman who should have known better—since she worked at the Mystic Marine Aquarium—once argued with me for an hour that dolphins are mammals. Although various porpoises, which are mammals, are known by the common name "dolphin," it is technically incorrect. The true dolphin, the hatchet-nosed dolphin, is a fish—not a mammal. It sometimes goes by the name *mahi-mahi* for commercial reasons.

This fish is very colorful, especially when fresh from the sea. A living rainbow at first, it quickly fades to a dull gray. It has a delicate and unique flavor. Unfortunately, the delicate flavor, like the vivid color, is short-lived. Broil the fresh fillets with a little garlic butter or try them Cracker Style (page 25). Don't freeze the fillets; the result is disappointing.

Marlin. One of the great game fishes of the world, often running well beyond the half-ton mark, marlin is sometimes offered either smoked or fresh in fish markets. Smoked marlin is a delicacy you probably won't find very often, as the fish is not yet widely known for eating. And as to fresh, a friend who had the opportunity to grill fresh marlin steaks maintains that they are excellent. My only question is, If you catch one of these monsters, what do you do with the extra thousand pounds or so of meat?

Swordfish. There is no problem in disposing of excess swordfish meat, even if the fish is many times the size of the hundred-pounder I caught last year. Almost everyone but me likes swordfish—I gave mine to the other fishermen on the boat.

The classic preparation is to bake the steaks in a 350° F oven with a little butter. Also try it sautéed with lots of onions.

Wolffish. Wolffish (catfish, ocean whitefish) is named for his formidable dentation—its teeth include large canines. Growing to lengths of up to 5 feet, wolffish are solitary bottom fish that prefer hard bottoms in cold, deep water. They eat primarily shellfish, crabs, and lobsters, so his meat reflects this, being one of the tastiest of all. With the possible exception of the mother-in-law fish, wolffish is probably the ugliest resident of the Gulf of Maine. The meat is delicate in texture and must be treated with care, but is well worth it. Don't expect to find him very often in the fish market, since even fishermen are not completely stupid. The largest specimen I ever saw weighed more than the forty-seven-pound codfish I caught the same day. On party boats it is very common for the anglers to all put money into a pool, which is awarded for the largest fish of the day. My codfish came at about eight in the morning—when we first started fishing—while the wolffish bit just before we left the fishing grounds to go home. The fisherman, who stood next to me for the whole trip, took home a pool of $760. I was not pleased.

Hake (Whiting). The temptation is great to call this fish by its New Jersey party boat name, "sewer trout," but who would try a recipe for sewer trout? Actually, the name is misleading, as the fish possesses a delicate flavor and texture that sends New Jersey anglers to sea at night in the depths of winter. The market euphemism *whiting* is less colorful but generally less accepted. There are several species of hake, of which only the silver hake is really entitled to the whiting label. All can be used in any of the cod recipes.

CAPTAIN TOM'S WOLFFISH

Serves 4

C aptain Tom Hill of the Yankee Fishing Fleet Out O' Gloucester graciously shared this recipe with me, which I only slightly modified by adding a little fresh lime juice. It is incomparable.

I N G R E D I E N T S

1/2 lime

2-3 pounds wolffish fillet

4 ounces Ritz crackers

2 tablespoons butter or margarine, melted

SOME

OCEAN

EXOTICS

Preheat the oven to 350° F. Wash the fish and pat dry with paper towels. Place the fillet on a baking rack over water in a baking dish. Squeeze the lime juice over the fillet and bake for about 5 minutes. Finely crumble the crackers (roll with a rolling pin between 2 sheets of wax paper or put through a food processor). Make a paste of the cracker crumbs and melted butter. Take the fish from the oven and cover it with the cracker paste. Return fish to oven and bake until it flakes on fork testing, approximately 10 minutes. If desired, brown the crust in the broiler for a few seconds.

BAKED STUFFED WOLFFISH

Serves 2

Hallelujah! Please follow this one closely.

I N G R E D I E N T S

1 tablespoon butter

1 tablespoon sesame or other light oil

1 tablespoon finely chopped fresh tarragon

8 ounces wolffish fillet

4 ounces Ritz crackers, crushed

4 ounces scallops, finely chopped

1/2 lime

P R O C E D U R E

Melt the butter in a large iron skillet, then add the oil and tarragon; stir for a few seconds over medium heat. Add the fish and sauté slowly for 3 minutes on each side. Set the oven to broil. Remove the fish and pour the butter over the crackers and scallops in a bowl. Mix well, then pack the stuffing over the fillet and put in the broiler for approximately 5 minutes to lightly brown the crust. Squeeze lime half over the fish and return to the broiler until the top is browned and crispy, another 5 minutes. Serve with plain rice, soy sauce, and Japanese vegetables.

STUFFED SEWER TROUT

Serves 4

I N G R E D I E N T S

1-1/2 pounds fresh hake fillets, sliced 1/4-inch thick

2/3 cup nonfat cottage cheese

1/3 cup seasoned bread crumbs

1/3 cup chopped fresh mushrooms

3—4 spinach leaves, lightly steamed

P R O C E D U R E

Preheat the oven to 350° F. Cover the oiled bottom of a glass baking dish with the fish fillets. Mix the cottage cheese, bread crumbs, and mushrooms to make a stuffing. Cover the fish with the stuffing and place the spinach leaves on top to prevent dehydration. Bake 15 minutes. Serve with tiny green peas and pearl onions.

HAKE WITH MUSHROOM-BROCCOLI STUFFING

Serves 2

Although the recipe is nominally for hake, any other mild white fish is also excellent.

I N G R E D I E N T S

1/2—1 pound hake fillets

1 small onion

1 tablespoon chopped green bell pepper

1 stalk celery, finely chopped

1 cup sliced fresh mushrooms

1/2–2/3 cup chopped cooked broccoli or spinach

1 cup stale bread crumbs

1 tablespoon butter, melted

1-1/2 tablespoons lemon juice

Grated Swiss cheese

P R O C E D U R E

Preheat the oven to 350° F. Coat a glass baking dish with non-stick vegetable oil spray. Cover the bottom of the dish with a single layer of fish fillets and set the dish in the refrigerator while you prepare the stuffing. Sauté the onion, green pepper, and celery until softened, about 3 minutes. Add the mushrooms and broccoli or spinach, and simmer for 5 minutes. Add the bread crumbs and blend the lemon juice into the butter. Pour the lemon butter over the fish, then cover with the stuffing. Sprinkle on the grated cheese. Bake until the fish flakes, 10 to 15 minutes.

OTHER SALTWATER FISH

In many species of fish the area surrounding the body cavity is poisonous or otherwise not too desirable—blowfish, goosefish, sea raven, sculpin, and sea robin come to mind. Blowfish tails are served in many finer restaurants as "sea squab," goosefish is called "monkfish"; the sea robin, sea raven, and sculpin remain anonymous.

Blowfish, or northern puffer, is perfectly safe but some of his southern relatives carry deadly toxins in the digestive tract; consequently, only the tail is eaten but it is delicious. Goosefish, or angler, has a flesh consistency closely related to half-set gelatin, which tends to lessen his table appeal to some. It lives on a diet of crab and lobster, and the taste of his flesh reflects this. The sea robin looks like some armored prehistoric monster, but the taste is quite modern—just beware of its spiny fins and body when cleaning. Likewise, the sculpin and sea raven have similar diets. Sea raven is probably the ugliest fish of all, but for some strange reason fishermen have dubbed it the mother-in-law fish. I have not tried toadfish—not because of possible poor flesh quality but because the spines are toxic—handling one is not healthy. Broiling is the commonest cooking method.

Anchovies, herring, sardines, capelin, silverside, and smelt are all eaten whole. Anchovies are primarily salted and dried. Herring—(whole or cut)—is principally marketed pickeled (see Chapter 21, on roughfish, for how to prepare this delightful dish), although canned herring sometimes appears in grocery stores. Canned sardines have, of course, been a staple for many years (again, refer to Chapter 21 for directions). Capelin, silverside, and smelt are either treated like sardines or cooked whole (roll in a mixture of cornmeal and flour then pan-fry).

FRESH

WATER

FINFISH

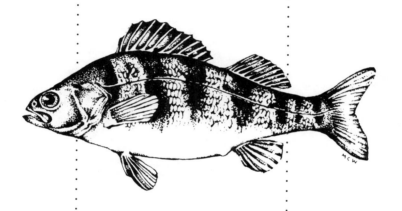

TWENTY

TROUT, SALMON, AND OTHER PANFISH

N ot everyone has access to the wealth of food in the oceans, but almost eveyone has access to freshwater fish. My wife's family is from West Texas, one of the driest places around, but they catch trout and catfish locally.

Perhaps it is because I was raised on the headwaters of one of the world's most renowned dry fly fishing streams that I have little use for the Salmonidae (trout family) today. A childhood diet of fresh-caught native trout pan-fried in bacon grease over a wood fire makes soft-fleshed, livery-tasking hatchery trout a mockery. And years of salmon loaf and patties (mix canned salmon, bread crumbs, and sautéed onions—bind with an egg and press into the desired form. Bake.) destroyed any incipient love for the larger cousin. There are many published recipes for these popular fish but here are a few of my favorites.

APACHE TROUT

An Apache friend once asked me why we don't utilize the native cedar trees here in the Northeast like they do back home in East Texas. It seems that his grandfather taught him this best way of preparing trout.

I N G R E D I E N T S

1 cleaned trout
Cedar bark

P R O C E D U R E

Build a fire in a pit lined with rocks.* When the rocks are hot, scrape out the ashes and coals to leave just the hot rocks. Wrap the cleaned fish in cedar bark and place it on the rocks. A burlap sack over the pit will help keep the heat in. Fish will be cooked after an hour or so. Fiddleheads (young ferns) and swamp cabbage are two spring greens that go well with this.

CAPE COD COOKOUT

Native Americans of the Cape Cod area taught the colonists a similar technique.

Dig a big hole in the sand. Line the hole with round rocks from well above the high tide line (see note below). Build a hot fire on the rocks. When the rocks are quite hot, scrape off the hot coals and ashes, then cover the rocks with wet seaweed. Add trout plus any clams, lobsters, or whatever else is desired, and cover with sea-

* Never use rocks from a stream, or where they have been exposed to water for some time. Water seeps into the rocks and, when the rocks are heated, turns to steam. Pieces of rock will fly for considerable distance when the steam pressure builds up enough. Please take my word for this; an experiment could be very dangerous.

weed. Spread burlap over the seaweed and cover with a couple inches of sand. Mark the site well, then go away for a couple of hours. When you come back the fish will be ready to eat; just scrape off the covering layers and dig in to some incredible eating. (Nowadays, we put corn on-the-cob in to cook with the fish and most people wash everything down with beer—hardly the most authentic, but tasty.)

ANCIENT AMERICAN BAKED TROUT

The people who lived in the western plains several thousand years ago, known to us as the "Old Ones," left pottery shards and even some complete pieces of very advanced pottery. Unfortunately, they left no written or oral records of where they went or who they became. From looking at their pottery, I guess that they were not strangers to the technique of wrapping a dressed fish in leaves, making a clay envelope around the leaves, and baking the whole in campfire ashes. The modern equivalent is Fish Terra-Cotta (page 24).

WOODS RUNNER TROUT

My New England woods ancestors had a pretty good approach. Build a fire enclosed by rocks with one rock having a flat surface that slopes gently into the fire. On the flat rock place wild onion and other suitable herbs, usually cress, sheep sorrel, or mint. The herbs season the cooking surface. Place the fish on the flat rock and cook 10 to 15 minutes. Generally it is best to turn the fish over once for even cooking, although I have watched real experts to whom this would be demeaning.

PAN TROUT

By the time I was a boy, older methods of cooking over an open fire or in a pit had been superseded by a European invention—the cast-iron pan. If "civilization" brought us one advantage, this has to be it. Try this slightly modernized recipe, passed down through my family for generations and still as relevant today as it was a hundred years ago.

INGREDIENTS

2–3 slices bacon

Fresh trout

1 part cornmeal

1 part all purpose flour

PROCEDURE

Properly, you should carry out this recipe with a wood fire in the deep woods, but you can also use the kitchen range and a (perish the thought) hatchery trout from the local supermarket, though a great deal is lost in translation.

Place the bacon in a cast-iron pan over medium heat. Render the bacon and set aside to drain on brown paper bags or paper towels. Make a mixture of half cornmeal and half flour, then roll the trout in this mixture, and fry in the bacon drippings. Brown it first on one side, then on the other, a total of 6 minutes. Note: For some real cadillac living, save part of the bacon drippings and use to make home fries with onions while the fish cooks. My grandfather used to start the day with fish and potatoes, accompanied by brewed coffee and a big slab of homemade apple pie. Considering the fact that most of his family lived into the nineties, this diet must not have been too bad.

PAN FISH PIQUANTE

Serves 4

Don't feel limited to such pan fish as perch, crappie, and bluegill; virtually any fish benefits from this treatment—just slice the fillets to about 1/4-inch thickness.

1–1-1/2 cups mayonnaise

1/2 cup lemon juice

1–2 pounds pan fish fillets, thinly sliced

1 cup sliced fresh mushrooms

1/4 pound hard cheese, grated

1 cup bread crumbs

Paprika

Fresh parsley

P R O C E D U R E

Preheat the oven to 350° F. Mix mayonnaise and lemon juice to make a sauce. Immerse the fish fillets in marinade and let marinate for 10 minutes. Lay the fish in a single layer in the bottom of a glass baking dish. Sprinkle the bread crumbs to just cover the fish. Layer with mushrooms and sprinkle with the cheese and paprika. Bake for 20 minutes. Remove from the oven and garnish with parsley. Serve with garlic bread and fresh spring vegetables.

MIXED FISH
SPRING CASSEROLE

Serves 3

One fine spring day the flounder (not a freshwater fish but so what?), yellow perch, and bluegills were all happily biting. The question was, What to do with about three pounds of mixed fillets that would fit two people and use all these species comfortably? I marinated the fillets in lemon juice for thirty minutes, dried them on paper towels, dipped them in beer batter (1 egg, 2 cups flour, 1 teaspoon baking powder, and 3/4 of a 12-ounce can of Michelob), and deep-fried them. They were excellent, but we could only eat half the fillets. The remaining half went into this casserole, since spring is also asparagus time.

I N G R E D I E N T S

1-1/2 pounds deep-fried fish fillets

Grated cheddar cheese

6 thick asparagus stalks, sliced
   in 1/8-inch discs

Preheat the oven to 350° F. Put the fillets in a shallow glass baking dish and cover with asparagus. Top with cheese and bake for 25 minutes.

SUNFISH

The ocean sunfish—moa moa—is the size of a medium fishing boat, but his closest relatives are the hand-size sunfish unique to eastern North America, such as bluegill, rock bass, pumpkinseed, and redfish. How this came about raises some interesting mechanical conjectures.

By now everyone is familiar with Louisiana blackened redfish. Redfish, a large freshwater sunfish, is seasoned with Creole herbs and seared until practically burned. Since Southern fish are usually much gamier than their Northern cousins, the heavy spices and herbs are not unexpected.

Most sunfish are relatively small—a one-pound fish is pretty much a rarity. This small size coupled with enormous scales largely accounts for its underutilization. The large scales tend to go everywhere when you clean the fish, making cleanup messy and extra rinsing necessary. But these problems are worth dealing with. The fish are easy to fillet and the meat is excellent.

All the pan fish recipes are applicable for sunfish, but here is a recipe particularly for these little fish.

CAJUN BLUEGILL

Try this for a delicious party hors d'oeuvre. Steam skinless, boneless bluegill fillets. Chill them and present on lettuce leaves over a bed of ice with

Louisiana Red Sauce (page 68). Don't be concerned about quantities; whatever amount you serve will disappear, regardless of the number of people involved.

PERCH

The perches, like catfish, have diversified into an enormous variety of fresh- and saltwater habitats. Yellow perch are the principal representative east of the Rocky Mountains, although white perch (primarily a saltwater dweller) has been successfully introduced to a number of lakes and streams. Yellow perch is highly prized in the Midwest. I recall seeing fillets for sale in Michigan for around $8 a pound, when codfish was only $2 or $3 a pound on the coast. Granted, codfish are a lot larger.

Simple to clean, fun to catch, and highly prolific, the yellow perch, *perca flavescens*, is probably the most delicious of all freshwater fish. Although always superb, it is at its best caught through the ice in winter. Usually I marinate the filleted fish in lemon juice and garlic for 30 minutes, dip them in beer batter, and deep-fry them. The French method of poaching in wine is an excellent alternative.

POACHED PERCH

Serves 3

INGREDIENTS

1 tablespoon vegetable oil
1 tablespoon margarine
Pinch of dry mustard
1 tablespoon soy sauce
1 tablespoon maple syrup

1 cup water

1/4–1/2 cup dry sherry

1 pound perch fillets

1 tablespoon cornstarch mixed with 1 tablespoon dry sherry

P R O C E D U R E

In a heavy, deep skillet over medium heat, put the oil and margarine and add mustard, soy sauce, maple syrup, water, and sherry. Bring to a boil, then lower the heat and simmer for about 5 minutes to blend the flavors. Put in the fish and poach until fish flakes when tested with a fork. Remove fish to a warmed platter. Add the cornstarch mixture to the poaching liquid, and cook, stirring constantly with a wire whisk, until liquid is thickened. Serve the fish with rice and pour sauce over them. Broccoli goes very well with this.

DEEP-FRIED PERCH

Serves 2 to 4

Have you ever wondered what kind of madness drives men out of a warm living room and onto frozen lakes in zero-degree temperatures with 30-knot winds? Last winter two of us drove up to within sight of the Canadian border on Lake Champlain, just to drill through twenty-seven inches of ice after yellow perch that seldom were longer than eight inches. Yellow perch are the very best when caught through a hole in the ice. The meat is firm but tasty with no pond taste. Fish living in warm freshwater often has a nasty muddy flavor. Ordinarily I avoid deep-frying but in this instance I just can't resist.

I N G R E D I E N T S

1–2 pounds perch fillets

Batter of choice (pages 22–23)

Put a large heavy pot over high heat. Add enough oil to fill the pot by about one-third and heat to a minimum of 375° F. Spread the fillets on towels. Adjust batter thickness with water to desired consistency—less liquid makes a thicker batter. The batter should be thick enough to coat the fillets but not absorb the cooking liquid. Coat the fillets with batter and drop individually into the hot oil. Cook a few at a time, so they have room to cook without sticking to each other. Turn the fillets once so they brown on both sides, about 2 minutes. Remove to paper towels or brown paper to drain. Serve with tossed salad green beans.

STIR-FRIED YELLOW PERCH

Serves 4

Here's an adaptation of a Chinese tradition.

I N G R E D I E N T S

1 pound perch fillets

2 tablespoons vegetable oil

1 10-ounce package frozen stir-fried vegetables

1 large dill pickle, thinly sliced

2 slices pineapple, or 2–3 teaspoons raisins

Dash of soy sauce

1 package crispy egg noodles

P R O C E D U R E

Steam or poach the perch fillets until they flake. Put a large cast-iron pan over medium heat and add the oil, then the vegetables. Stir-fry the vegetables, crumpling the fillets into the mix. Add the pickle and break up the pineapple or raisins into the dish. Sprinkle with soy sauce. Serve over crispy egg noodles.

BAKED YELLOW PERCH FILLETS

Serves 4

Do not overbake. The fillets are small and delicate.

INGREDIENTS

1-1/2 pounds perch fillets

1/2 cup mayonnaise or beaten egg whites

1 cup seasoned bread crumbs or cracker crumbs

3–4 teaspoons (1/2 stick) butter, melted

2 teaspoons lemon juice

PROCEDURE

Preheat the oven to 350° F. Rinse and dry the fillets. Dip the fillets in the mayonnaise or egg whites and roll in the bread or cracker crumbs; layer in an oiled glass baking dish. Sprinkle with butter and lemon juice. Bake 20 minutes. Accompany with lima beans and mashed sweet potatoes.

SAUTÉED YELLOW PERCH FILLETS

Serves 3

INGREDIENTS

2 tablespoons (1/4 stick) margarine

2 tablespoons chopped onion

12 perch, 7–9 inches long

PROCEDURE

In a large cast-iron pan, melt the margarine. Add the onion and continue cooking until the onion is transparent, about 3 minutes. Add the fillets and cook until the fish flakes apart, about 5 minutes.

YELLOW PERCH À LA RITZ

Serves 4

I N G R E D I E N T S

8 ounces Ritz crackers

2 teaspoons tarragon, finely chopped or powdered

1 teaspoon chopped fresh dill

2 tablespoons finely chopped onion

1 pound yellow perch fillets

1/2 cup (1 stick) butter or margarine

5 tablespoons lemon juice

Garlic powder to taste

P R O C E D U R E

Preheat the oven to 350° F. Saute the onions until softened, or microwave with a little butter for 2 minutes. Crumble the crackers into a medium bowl along with the tarragon, dill, and onion. Fill the bottom of an oiled glass baking dish with a single layer of fillets. Melt the butter and the lemon juice. Add to the cracker mix and stir to a paste. Sprinkle the fish with garlic powder and cover with the cracker mix. Bake for 15 minutes. Accompany with French-style green beans and boiled potatoes.

CATFISH

. . . .

Fresh and salt waters in most of the world host catfish. There is a mountain lake in Vermont where the ice usually breaks up by July 4, that contains the best brown bullheads I have ever seen. The enormous white and sail catfish of Tampa Bay make great fish cakes. Hundred-pound-plus yellow catfish of the Mississippi are pursued for chowder and catfish gumbo.

All of the American catfish I've encountered have three nasty spines—two pectorals (side) and a dorsal (back). Care is the word for handling them. Grasp them with your thumb behind one pectoral, the dorsal between first and second fingers, and the third and fourth fingers behind the other pectoral. This way the fish cannot spine you, since the spines are on the leading edge of the fins. It is not fun to be spined. I had a white catfish bounce off a cement pier in the Florida Keys and land on my right leg by its dorsal spine. My leg recovered after only two weeks.

Whether brown bullhead, white catfish, sail catfish, or the giant yellow catfish of the Mississippi River, the meat is good. Since catfish are so hardy, they are probably the most widely raised commercial fish crop. Some aquaculturalists raise only catfish for market. The meat is adaptable to most recipes, from whole fried fish to fish cakes. Since my wife's former home was New Orleans, catfish gumbo ranks high in our book. The recipe for this delight is given on page 39.

CATFISH CROQUETTES

When catfish get large they can become very tough—especially the sailcats commonly caught in Florida. These fish are delicious, so the trick is to use them in such a way as to avoid the old-tire texture while retaining the flavor. Tenderizing is simple; just put boneless catfish fillets through a grinder. Catfish can be used in fish cake recipes or made into a croquette served with a white cream sauce.

INGREDIENTS

1 cup cooked ground catfish
1/2–1 cup leftover rice, vegetables, potatoes, or whatever else is in the refrigerator
1 tablespoon mild onion, minced
1 large egg
3/4 cup plus 1 tablespoon milk
1/2 cup plus 2 tablespoons all-purpose flour
1 cup seasoned bread crumbs or cracker crumbs
2 tablespoons (1/4 stick) margarine

Preheat oven to 450° F. Combine the catfish with the rice or vegetables and onion; mix well. Form into cakes or balls and refrigerate for 20 minutes.

Melt margarine in a heavy skillet, blend in 2 tablespoons flour with a wire whisk, and cook for 2 minutes to remove the raw flour taste. Slowly add the 3/4 cup milk, stirring constantly until thickened.

Take the cakes out of the refrigerator, dip in egg beaten with tablespoon of milk, and roll in the crumbs. Place cakes on a baking sheet and bake for 10 minutes or until browned.

Note: If you made cone-shaped lumps or blobs, they are called croquettes and are served with this thick white sauce. If you made patties, you can put them between slices of bread spread with tartar sauce and have a better fish sandwich than you'll find at a fast-food emporium.

CALICO BASS

Calico bass (strawberry bass, crappie) is another very common pan fish of sunfish shape, although slightly larger. The meat of a calico is very soft and must be handled carefully, but the taste is very good if the environment is favorable. Warm, sluggish rivers produce foul-tasting crappies (is the name a coincidence?), but the strawberry bass from cold, deep lakes, such as Champlain and a local I refuse to name, are excellent.

Generally, the fish are too thin for broiling, but most other methods are fine. Water is the best liquid for poaching. Avoid heavy herbs and spices in any stuffing or breading. Fish chowder is better made with perch or saltwater fish. My favorite preparation is deep-frying with batter.

WALLEYE PIKE

Actually a large member of the perch family, the walleye lives strictly in colder waters such as those in Canada. To my mind this is the best of all freshwater fish. Not only is "old marble eyes" the best eating, it is fun to catch and easy to clean.

The only preparation I have ever seen is pan sautéing, although almost any other way should be fine. Walleyes are eaten pretty much where they are caught, so elaborate cooking has never developed.

183

TROUT,
SALMON,
AND OTHER
PANFISH

CHAMPLAIN WALLEYE

Serves 4

2–3 strips bacon

1 cup cornmeal

1 cup all-purpose flour

2 pounds walleye fillets

P R O C E D U R E

Fry the bacon in a heavy pan until browned, about 10 minutes. Drain on paper towels or brown paper. Mix the cornmeal and flour together, then roll the fillets in the mix to coat well. Sauté in the bacon drippings until fish flakes, about 5 minutes. Serve fish with crumbled bacon, a green vegetable, and pasta.

OTHER FRESH WATER FISH

Suckers. The common brown sucker cohabitates with trout, but obviously trout get all the attention. This is a mistake. In the spring, while the waters are still cold, suckers are just as good eating as trout. It is only when waters get warm that suckers develop worms, principally along the backbone.

The major departure from trout is the scales. Instead of the miniscule trout scales, suckers have large, inedible scales. The scales overlap from head to tail just like house shingles, for similar reasons. Stroke the fish from tail to head with an edged instrument to catch and remove the scales. Otherwise treat exactly like trout. The other major problem with the sucker family is Y bones (discussed on page 11).

Suckers have very soft meat; thus to pan-fry, the coating mix must be very dry. Use a half-and-half mix of whole-wheat flour and cornmeal, with a touch of baking powder to puff the crust. First roll the scored fillets in the coating mix, then set aside for 30 minutes. The first coating will almost disappear, so reroll the fish in the mixture. Now pan-fry the fillets until just tender, about 3 minutes.

Minnows and Dace. Bones, bones, and more bones. The meat of these fish would undoubtedly be good, but the work involved is just too much. I tried a large dace on a mountain camping trip once. Don't bother.

Large- and Smallmouth Bass. Except to a fisherman who really likes eating these fish, the distinction is of no significance. Personally, I won't eat either unless I catch it ice fishing. The meat is fine battered and deep-fried when the fish is taken from very cold water, but tastes muddy when from warmer waters. Bassophiles claim that baked stuffed smallmouth is a worthy dish; they can keep it.

Common Eel. Any fisherman who has caught one of these snakelike fish at night—the usual time to encounter them—will tell you, usually with colorful metaphor, just how easy it is to get them off the hook. These fish are highly flexible and slimy, and they delight in winding themselves around your fishing line, arm, or anything else handy. Their bite is insignificant and their fins are soft, but their slither and slime dissuade most people from more intimate acquaintance. It's really too bad, since they are an excellent fish—useful as a thickener in soup, excellent fried, and incomparable smoked. Europeans so appreciate eel that they transport the young to inland lakes the fish could not otherwise reach.

If you plan to fry the eel, cut it into 1- to 1-1/2-inch pieces. Longer pieces curl up in the pan while cooking, making irregular doneness as well as freaking out those of gentler nature. Smoke the fish whole (skin but leave the head on).

Pickerel and pike. To the untrained eye, these freshwater barracuda look alike, with only small differences in their markings. The big difference is the bone structure. Pickerel have nasty little Y-shaped bones through their flesh that are lacking in pike. Treatment of the fish varies accordingly, even though they are equally delicious. Pike can be filleted and cooked by almost any method, but pickerel requires special care unless you care to pick bones out of your teeth. Pickling, as with herring, softens the bones (gefilte fish). Cuisinarting also gives an excellent basis for fish cakes. There is even one man on the Canadian border of New York State who can cut boneless chunks of meat from a pickerel—impressive.

Arctic Char and Whiting. These fish live in such cold waters that I have not yet had a chance to sample them. According to all I have heard, they can be treated like trout.

Smelt. There are people who sneer at these little fish, saying they are only fit for bait. But there are also people who feel that shrimp are only fit for bait. Having eaten lake trout and the warm-water fishes caught with shrimp, I much prefer to eat the bait.

Although smelt are caught in either fresh or salt water, pan-frying is the only preparation method I have seen. They are rolled in flour and sautéed in bacon grease or butter.

Fresh-water smelt are netted on their spawning run in late February or March, while saline smelt are hook-and-lined from the docks in late fall. Cleaning of either is simple and unique to this fish. Small fish—less than about 4 or 5 inches—are eaten whole. Larger fish are decapitated with a twist of the wrist and eviscerated with a flick of the thumb. If that sounds a little rough, consider that hamburger is the macerated flesh of a castrated bovine.

TWENTY-ONE

ROUGH FISH

There are a number of species of both fresh and salt-water fish that are grouped under the heading "rough." The term is used to describe non-sport, noncommercial fishes that are generally not sought for human consumption. But what a big mistake it is to not eat these fish. "If it swims, it's edible" is the way one old-timer put it to me—and I agree. Properly handled and prepared, almost any fish is good to eat. This big bugaboo of preparation and handling is really a false alarm. A call or letter to your local agricultural extension service (or state fish and game commission) will net you more information about a particular fish than you would believe exists. The universities of Wisconsin and South Dakota, for example, have prepared extremely fine booklets detailing the preparation of many rough fish such as carp, sucker, gar, and bowfin. The University of Bridgeport, Connecticut, Institute for Anguilliform Research publishes a comprehensive booklet on eel cookery.

The single most common complaint regarding most rough fish concerns their bones. Intermuscular (or Y) bones abound in the sucker, carp, and pickerel families of fresh water (they are in trout also, but people tolerate these bones) and in the herring and porgie families of salt water. There are a variety of ways to get by these bones. Unless you have the patience to pick the bones out of cooked or raw flesh, there are four common attacks: (1) pickle the fish (the bones soften), (2) can the fish (the necessary 10–15 pounds of pressure softens the bones), (3) twice-grind the meat to destroy the bones (for fish cakes, loaf, or sausage), (4) score the fillets every 1/4 inch so that the cooking oil or sauce will penetrate and soften the bones.

The second major complaint—soft flesh—is even more easily dealt with. Either freeze the fillets overnight or pack them in salt for a day or so. This will firm them amazingly.

Sometimes fish such as carp will have a strong taste, which is a common third complaint. Remove the skin and dark flesh at once and most of the strong flavor will be removed with it. But remember, a fish is literally what it eats, so take fish only from clear and unpolluted waters so that the flesh will be unadorned by civic and industrial pollutants.

There are only two absolute no-nos about rough fish other than the obvious caution against polluted waters. First, do not, under any circumstances, eat gar eggs; they are deadly poison. Second, do not use any part of the body contents from any of the puffer fish; some contain deadly toxins and only a specialist can tell you which, so it is safest to avoid them all.

Here are a few of the rough fish and how to handle them. Since these are not fish you can just go to the local supermarket and buy in convenient quantities, it didn't make much sense to specify serving portions. Cook what you catch or are given. As with any other fish, a serving of meat is from a quarter to a half pound, so choose your guest list to fit the fish, not the reverse.

CARP

Europeans and Asians alike prize carp. The fish is not so widely treasured by Americans because of its strong flavor, often caused by warm or polluted waters, and the abundance of intermuscular bones. Most of the strong flavor resides in the dark meat and the mud vein that lies along the lateral line of the fish. Removing the dark parts also gets rid of most of the objectionable taste. Take carp only from cold waters. Remove the bones as outlined above.

Smoked Carp

Because carp is a naturally fatty fish, smoking is a prime method of preparation.

INGREDIENTS

Carp fillets

Marinade (1/4 cup noniodized salt to 1 gallon water)

Optional seasonings (honey, thyme, brown sugar)

PROCEDURE

It is best to smoke fish with the skin intact so that the meat is kept together, but carp have huge scales. "Fleecing" is the process used to remove scales without damaging the skin. Insert the edge of a sharp, thin knife blade under a row of scales at the tail of the fish and work it back and forth while pulling it slowly forward. This will, with a little practice, lift the scales away while leaving the skin intact.

Fillet the carp fleecing, then marinate from 1 hour to overnight. The length of time and strength of the marinade are crucial to the final product. The marinade here is a light taste that won't appeal to everyone. I also rinse the fillets after marinating, while others may not. Popular additions to the marinade are brown sugar, honey, thyme, and maple syrup. Brushing these on the smoke-ready fillets is another common ploy.

Place the fillets on the smoking rack skin side down and put in the smoker. Smoke with hickory, mesquite, apple, or maple chips to the desired doneness. The time to smoke depends on two factors—the thickness of the fish and the temperature of the smoker (see SMOKING, page 16, for further details). The fish should be tender but not leathery.

Hungarian Baked Carp

INGREDIENTS

1 small onion

1 tablespoon vegetable oil

1 teaspoon paprika

1 cup fish stock

1/2 cup sour cream at room temperature, or plain nonfat yogurt

P R O C E D U R E

Preheat the oven to 300° F. Score the fillets every 1/4 inch so that the sauce can penetrate and soften the Y bones. Place the fillets in a single layer in a clear glass baking dish. Chop and partly cook the onion in the oil to soften (about 2 minutes in a microwave on high). Place the softened onion, oil, paprika, and stock in a medium saucepan and blend over low heat for about 5 minutes. Remove from the heat and blend in the sour cream or yogurt slowly to make a sauce.

Pour the sauce over the fish and bake until the fish flakes easily, about 30 minutes. Spaetzle (Galuska, in Hungarian) is the usual accompaniment. Grandma Soltesz's traditional method of preparing Galuska is:

I N G R E D I E N T S

2 eggs   Flour

P R O C E D U R E

Beat eggs in a bowl and work in sifted flour to form a rubbery dough. Roll the dough out as thin as you can, slice into 1/4-thick pieces and cook until they float on top. Drain the noodles and fry in melted butter. Serve plain with the carp or mix with green beans for another tempting treat.

SHEEPSHEAD— PAUPERS LOBSTER 1

Voila! A dish that tastes much like lobster from a rough fish. Sheepshead (freshwater drum) is another surprisingly underutilized freshwater fish—without Y bones. It is an easy fish to fillet and makes excellent chowder, but one of the simplest and best ways to treat the meat is Pauper's Lobster.

Sheepshead fillets
Melted butter
Lemon juice

P R O C E D U R E

Drop 1/2-inch-thick pieces of fish into boiling water and cook until tender, about 4 minutes. Drain well. Add lemon juice to butter and dip the pieces. Alternatively, poach the fillets.

BURBOT— PAUPER'S LOBSTER 2

B urbot (freshwater cusk) is another undervalued fish that lends itself to the same treatment as sheepshead. However, the fish is found only in far northern lakes, where it is resoundingly hated for its preferred diet of yellow perch eggs. Incidentally, the fish spawns under ice—a rather unique and chilly idea. Follow the same process as for sheepshead.

MARINATED BROILED CARP

I N G R E D I E N T S

Carp fillets
Lemon or grapefruit juice
1 part soy sauce

1 part lime juice
Melted butter
Paprika
Basil

P R O C E D U R E

Marinate the fillets in citrus juice (lemon for suckers, grapefruit for pike) for at least 30 minutes. Place the fillets in a broil pan and add butter, paprika, basil, and any other garnishes desired. Broil fillets until they flake easily, about 4 minutes. Be cautious—overcooking gives a tough and rather tasteless product.

MOCK SALMON

Carp makes an excellent substitute for expensive canned salmon. Be sure to read the section on CANNING on page 00 before proceeding.

I N G R E D I E N T S

Carp fillets, skinned and deveined
Brine (1/2 cup noniodized salt to 1 gallon water)
1 part olive oil
2 parts distilled white vinegar
2 parts ketchup or tomato sauce

P R O C E D U R E

Soak fillets fish overnight in the brine. Rinse in fresh water and cut into pieces small enough to pack into half-pint canning jars. Wash and sterilize the jars and their lids. Keep jars and lids hot. Mix the oil, vinegar, and ketchup or tomato sauce in a bowl.

Pack the fish solidly into the hot jars to within about 1 inch of the top. Cover the fish with the canning mixture, eliminating air pockets by running the blade of a knife down the inside of the jar. Leave about 3/4 inch headspace and cover the jars loosely. Place in pressure canner with about 1/2 inch water and bring to a boil. Boil for a couple of minutes, then tighten the jar lids and cover the canner. Process according to directions. Begin timing when the pressure is up to the chosen 10 or 15 pounds, and keep it there for the full time. *Do not deviate from the times and pressures recommended; botulism is fatal.* After the desired time, turn off heat and let the canner cool naturally. Store the jars in a cool, dark place.

DEEP-FRIED CARP

Score the fillets every 1/4 inch to allow penetration of the cooking oil. Carp is an oily fish, so any coating for frying must be very dry.

INGREDIENTS

Vegetable oil, for deep-frying
Carp fillets, scored
1 part cornmeal
1 part whole-wheat flour
1 part all-purpose flour

Pinch of baking powder
Milk or beaten egg
Paprika
Fresh dill

PROCEDURE

Heat oil to at least 375° F. Mix cornmeal, flours, baking powder, paprika, and dill. Dip fish in milk or beaten egg, then roll in the flour mixture. Drop fish pieces into hot oil and fry until brown, about 2 mintues. Drain on paper towels or brown paper.

PICKLING ROUGH FISH

For herring, suckers, carp, and pike, pickling has always been a popular way of softening the bones to make eating the fish a more pleasurable experience.

Pickling is not for long-term preservation, but it works well for several weeks if the fish is kept refrigerated, and even longer if also canned. There are basically two pickling methods: hot pack and cold pack. Cold pack pickles raw fish, while hot pack cooks the fish.

I N G R E D I E N T S

Fish fillets
First pickling solution:
> Vinegar
> Noniodized salt

Second pickling solution:
> 3/4 cup sugar
> 1 quart wine vinegar
> Pickling spices to taste

Additions:
> Vegetables
> Yogurt or sour cream

C O L D   P A C K   P R O C E D U R E

Freeze the fish for several weeks to kill bacteria, then soak in the first pickling solution for 5–7 days, depending on how large the fish pieces are. The bones will disolve during this period, so don't cut the time short.

Rinse the fish in cold water and repack in the second pickling solution. Start with about 1/8 teaspoon of pickling spices (or dill and tarragon) to 1 quart liquid and adjust to taste. Add onion slices, cauliflower or broccoli florets, carrot slices, or small whole beets, as desired. Let sit for 1 week before you try it; if not sufficiently cured, keep until flavor develops properly.

H O T   P A C K   P R O C E D U R E

Score the fillets and steam until they flake, about 4 minutes. Place in the first pickling solution for 1 week so the bones soften. Rinse with cold water and pack in the second pickling solution and let sit for 1 week. Try serving with yogurt or sour cream instead of the brine juice.

193

ROUGH

FISH

RECIPE INDEX

197

RECIPE
INDEX